PERCEPTIONS IS EVERYTHING

Authored By: Ras Strength,
Preface By: Ras Jah GoGo
Introduction By: Bro. Albert X
SOLOMON & MAKEDA PUBLISHING |

Copyright © 2016 by Solomon & Makeda Publishing

All Rights Reserved. No Parts of this book may be reproduced in any form without the express written consent of Publisher/Author, except in the case of brief quotations embodied within relevant articles and book reviews for print and electronic media.

PREFACE

First, let's open with the fact that symbols are signs that stand for an object or idea. Symbols and their concepts include many different levels of interpretations. A symbol, in its intermediary function, expresses a transitional meaning that gives it interpretative connection with various other emblems, signs, gestures, and pictures.

What will be interesting to know is the affect that the symbols, pictures, and signs have had on us and our lives. The different forms and levels of the experience of and relationship the symbol has to reality grows and changes as we do. In this writing the concept of analogy is also very important.

Symbols are basic complex artistic forms and gestures conveying concepts. Iconography uses conventional or traditional wisdoms to represent divine beings and spirits. The two are required for truth to be added to either's use and/or meaning.

Now the word symbol comes from the Greek symbolon, which means contract, token, insignia, and means of identification. For example, the locks on the Crown (head) of a Rasta identifies and symbolizes his/her "Way of Life".

Nations and religions use pictorial symbols to identify themselves and express their ideals. Symbols such as flags, stop signs, or the colors of a Rastafari Crown are visual. The inventions of symbols rank among our oldest and most basic abilities, an example would be the letters of the alphabet or the Great Pyramids.

Look at the many forms of experience associated with sacred or holy symbols. The origin of many such symbols or figures indicates an identity beyond, and can be used as a mark to point out the sacred and holy. Symbolic representation should be viewed from this aspect.

Every time a symbol is engaged it will bring about a renewed actualization and a continual remembrance of a revelation. A Most sacred stone, plant, drum, human body, totem symbol or pictures of ancestors all represent the sacred or holy and guarantee its presence and efficacy.

An example of this is when I would go to my friends and neighbor's houses and see pictures hanging on walls, on top of tables, with pretty frames. I took it upon myself to ask questions about the objects and expressions. One of the questions I asked was who are those people hanging on the wall? I was then told that the pictures, and some of the figures on the pictures, was of her husband and other family members. So I started to identify with the man; and the other people that I had seen in my earlier years in similar pictures in my own house. I asked my mother was the man in one of the many pictures my father, and was those other people my family? She then told me no and that the man was her boss and the other people were co-workers. She showed me a book with various pictures and said you see this man, pointing to a figure on one of the pictures, that's your father right there, and she began to reveal to me pictures of my many ancestors. So I know intimately that pictures have profound effects on individuals. A simple visit to a friend's house made me feel like a part of that family. So it is with pictures, symbols, images, ect., that we as human beings come in contact with. This is why we need to take care of what we allow in our presence, into our perceptions, and into our minds.

Ras Jah GoGo

INTRODUCTION

This is a book written about Symbolism, Iconography, Phonography, Imagery. In this context I want to convey what the above subject has in common with Social Influences. Social Influences are what we learn from the time we are born, up to this very moment, from members of our family, friends, other human beings, our community, and the lingering affect it has on us as individuals. As babies, we were born into "this" world knowing nothing. From the time we are born to when we're approximately seven years old we learn largely unconsciously from our parents. From the ages of 8 to 13 is when we learn by consciously and unconsciously copying friends. Some of our most important values - core values are formed when we're around 10 years old-are established during this phase. From the ages of 14 to 21 years, we acquire values that affect our relationship to people and maybe our environment. Let me give an example: What kind of detergent do you use to wash clothing, is it Tide, Gain, or Ajax? Did you make a choice based on the quality of the detergent? If that's not the case, why did you make that selection? Could it be because when you grew up as a child a particular detergent was used in the home? If that be the case, then the use of that detergent is an example of a symbol of Social Influence. While some of the symbols and images we learned as children, as well as in adulthood, where empowering, unfortunately some of them limit the way we think and hold us back. It's a fact that the knowledge we have has come to us through Social Influences and were taught to us through Images and Symbols.

Idolatry is something that, because of its natural properties, historical associations, or mere convention, has come to be understood as referring beyond itself to some other reality. Virtually anything can become idolatry, not only objects but actions and gestures (A gesture is something that takes the place of words in communicating a thought or feeling, a gesture is also an expression).

Idolatry is a pictorial representation: An image, or a mental representation of anything not actually presented to the senses. Everything that is manifested was first a mental picture and was brought into expression by the forming power of the imagination. Man accumulates a mass of ideas about substance and life, and with his imagination he molds them into shape.

In the quest to know Thy True Self, it would be wise to begin a purging process that would burn away the dross. which leads us to understanding the deepest and most influential ways a Symbol, which has become an idol, decreases righteousness.

Our conscious mind has a plethora of known and unknown, productive and unproductive symbols, that not only come into being and grow, they eventually wither and die if, in changed historical circumstance, they can no longer perform their work as they did in the past.

While at the same time, our subconscious mind has the ability to store negative images that can have a stronghold on us and stifle our journey and progress. It is through observation, and Focal Consciousness, that we must learn how to identify when we're being subtlety influenced by the negative actions that have been passed down to us through traditions; that we operate on as Truth understanding that yesterday's Truth may not have the power to deal with today's reality.

Idolatry both in the Bible and in modern usage, is ambiguous. The term ranges in meaning from the narrow sense of offering sacrifice and prayer to a material representation of an "idol", to the broad sense of treating as of ultimate importance some person, thing, or concept other than God. Idolatry is also the worship of a physical object as a god, especially, such worship of a made image. We are often tempted to worship such idols as the false gods of greed, covetousness, jealousy, retaliation, and other forms of negation.

Idolatry, being explained here, is a material form representing an idea, and it is not idolatry to make idols and worship with them, if the heart understands their significance. But if the understanding is without love, mere intellectual perception, then man "knowth not yet as he ought to know." Those who have love, the love of God quickened in their hearts, are not disturbed by idols. It makes no difference to them how many representatives there are of God, because their inmost being, the very heart of their existence, is centered in the consciousness of the One. The fact is that every form and shape in existence is representative of God.

Today the scholars who study ancient and modern religions do not use the term idolatry, but the word generally means giving someone or something other than God devotion that should belong only to Him. This subject is vast and detailed. It is Our hopes that this writing begins a process of removing the misconceptions of reality that have been clandestinely, subtly, and strategically placed over our mind's eye; that prevents us from seeing through the murky maze of deception. We need to come to the realization that we have been reared to envision reality from the standpoint of a surface dweller, a face value believer, and ones that allows others to interpret reality for us: without a thorough investigation, that is based on documented and proven facts, this could be shocking. Especially when misconception is a concern, and that misconception seems like betrayal. It is our desire to bring about a work of the deepest concepts of truth, for an increase in knowledge, wisdom, and understanding of reality in a way that is digested smoothly and comprehensible.

Bro. Albert X

PERCEPTIONS
IS
EVERYTHING

To trace the origin, development, and differentiation of a symbol is a complicated process. Almost every symbol and picture in religion is at first either directly or indirectly connected with the sense impressions and objects of man's environment. Many are derived from the objects of nature, and others are artificially constructed in a process of intuitive perception, emotional experience, or rational reflection. In most cases, the constructions are again related to objects in the world of sense perception. A tendency toward simplification, abbreviation into signs, and abstraction from sense objects is quite evident, as well as a tendency to concentrate several processes into a single symbol. A good example of this last tendency may be seen in ancient Christian portrayals of the triumphant cross before a background of a star-filled heaven that appear in the apses of many basilican churches. In these representations, the Crucifixion, Resurrection, Ascension, exaltation, and Transfiguration of Christ are joined to apocalyptic concepts (centering on sudden interventions by God into history) inherent in the doctrine of the Last Judgment. An excellent example of such an apse mosaic is to be found in the St. Apollinaire in Classe, near Ravenna (in Italy). On the other hand, there is a tendency to accumulate, combine, multiply, and differentiate symbolical statements for the same thought or circumstance, as seen, for example, on the sarcophagi (stone coffins) of late Christian antiquity-especially in Ravenna. Here, the same idea is symbolically expressed in various manners; e.g., by means of persons, objects, animals, and signs, all appearing side by side.

The forms and figures of symbolical thought can change into exaggerations and rank growths, however, and lead to transformations and hybrids-figures with several heads, faces, or hands-as exemplified in the statues and pictorial representations of the deities of India (e.g., the multi-armed goddess Kali) and of Slavic tribes (e.g., the four-headed Suantevitus). The meaning of individual symbols can change and even be perverted. The lamb that in ancient Christian art symbolizes Christ may also symbolize the Apostles or mankind in general. The dove may symbolize the Holy Spirit or the human soul. The wheel or circle can symbolize the universe, the sun, or even the underworld. The Encyclopaedic Christian allegorism (symbolism) of the Middle Ages offers many interesting examples, as noted in the writings of Isadore of Seville, a 6th- to 7th-century Spanish theologian, and Rabanus Maurus, a 9th-century German abbot and encyclopaedist.

The foundations of the symbolization process lie in the areas of the conscious and the unconscious, of experience and thought, and of sense perception, intuition, and imagination. From these arises the structure of religious symbolism. Sensation and physiological and psychological processes participate in the formation of the symbol structure. Extraordinary religious experiences and conditions, visions, ecstasy, and religious delirium brought about by intoxication, hallucinogenics, or drugs that produce euphoria and changes in consciousness must also be taken into consideration. The symbol itself, however, is intended as an objective concentration of experiences of the transcendent world and not as a subjective construction of a personally creative process. In cultic and mystical visions and trances, the forms and processes of the external world and of the religious tradition are condensed and combined with mythical images and historical events and take on a life of their own. The process of rational conceptualization and structuralization, however, also plays a part in the origin and development of many symbols. There is a correlation between sense perception, imagination, and the work of the intellect.

Any attempt to find a place for imagination in faith, religion, or theology will encounter major problems from the start. Imagination has been regulated to the realm and science of psychology, and has not been defined properly enough to receive any other designation for expanded use. For example, the King James Version of the Bible, which was to set a standard of English usage for some three hundred and fifty years, translated three Hebrew words - "Yeser" (Gen. 8:21, Dut. 31:21), "Sheriruth" (Jer. 3:17, 7:24 & 11:8), and "Mahashebeth" (Provo 6:18, Lam. 3:60); and three Greek words "Dialogismos" (Rom. 1: 21), "Dianoia" (Luke 1: 51), and "Logismos" (2 Cor. 10:5) - all by the single English word "Imagination". This is a very deceptive error that hides the true intent of corruption by the translators. In each case the intent is pejorative, tending to make worse or degenerating, of the English word "Imagination", so that while none of the modern translations retain King James' usage, centuries of evil associations cannot be readily sloughed off. In the Calvinist Protestant churches, formed in various continental European countries, it was reiterated that "God rejects without exception all shapes and pictures, and other symbols by which the superstitious believe they can bring Him near to them. These images defile and insult the Majesty of God". Never mind that it was the imagery of the Cross, gained through the imaginative faculty of Constantine I (the Great Roman Empire 306-337), that gave Christianity's origin a residence in this world in the first place.

The suspicion of images thereby engendered in that tradition expressed itself subsequently in architecture, styles of worship, and in a highly-conceptualized form of articulation which sought to reduce image-type thinking on the part of theologians. Any further probability of associating religion or theology with imagination met its most serious discouragement from such statements as those of George W. F. Hegal, said to be the greatest of the German idealist philosophers, and one of the most fertile minds in the history of European thought, that "Theism in all its forms is an imaginative distortion of final Truth"; or Ludwig Feuerbach, German philosopher, assailant of Christianity, and predecessor of Marxism's rejection of God that "What has been called the mythopoeic function of imagination creates the object of religion, which in that act stands revealed as delusion"; or latterly of Jean-Paul Sartre, French philosopher, playwright, novelist, an essayist, best known as one of the leaders of twentieth-century atheistic existentialism, that "The art of imagination is a magical one. It is an incantation designed to produce the object of one's thought, the thing one desires, in a manner that one can take possession of it. I can stop the existence of the unreal object of imagination at any time". Having these pronouncements from the early 1800's to the late 1900's attempted to make certain that any enlightenment, that could be gained through the imagination faculty, would be done so under the strain and pressure of doubt and ridicule.

From imagination, which is a faculty and not just an aspect of thinking, the opposite may be true, we conjure symbols. Paul Ricoeur, French philosopher who has written widely on religion and theology, celebrated dictum, Le symbole donne a penser, says, "The symbol gives us the date, or the stimulus, or both, for thinking". Here is where imagination begins to manifest its works into this world, and into Life. Ricoeur's description of symbol defines it as the cause of thought towards whatever the symbol stands for, or represent. This point will be keenly realized later on in this writing.

The symbol, verbal, visual, ritual or whatever, represents in ordered form certain aspects of the world, but also, by so doing, sets a certain distance between the world and the Self: it both organizes the immediacy of experience and makes it strange. It proposes structures for understanding and so too suggests questions to be asked. This is true at the level of social ideology, and at the level of individual psychological development (hence in the psychoanalytic context, the significance of the stage of object-formation and the beginning of object- relationship).

Of course, this does not imply that symbols are mysteriously given: they are formed. But the point is that they are not formed by the imagination of individuals who are already quite clear about what they want to say and need only a better way of saying it. Their formation is itself the beginning of a process of understanding, bringing something into language. They remain so that others may travel a familiar path as they navigate the journey also. As modern linguists and anthropologists insist, the very structure of various languages already contain symbolic responses to the world's hidden symbolic cosmologies. With such view accepted, the development of symbolism in religious language is not a process of the encrustation of an original, a simple idea with distracting and extraneous illustration or ornament. Like all other serious human discourses, religious language requires a symbolic foundation. But equally, we should beware of a naive evolutionism which sees the development of religious language as a progressive emancipation from myth and metaphor; this would imply that there might, in the long run, be a form of consciousness which could bypass symbols of any kind. A very problematic idea, and one which characteristically belongs with a particular view of the mind's absolute freedom from social conditioning.

Symbolism, the basic and often complex artistic forms and gestures used as a kind of key to convey religious concepts, and iconography; the visual, auditory, and kinetic representations of religious ideas and events, have been utilized by all the religions of the world, with no exceptions.

The symbolic character of religion has often been stressed over in attempts to present religion rationally. The symbolic aspect of religion is even considered by some scholars of psychology and mythology as the main characteristic of religious expression. Scholars of comparative religions, ethnologist, and psychologist have gathered and interpreted a great abundance of material on the symbolical aspects of religion, especially in relation to Eastern and Primitive religions. In recent Christian theology and liturgical practices another revaluation of religious symbolical elements has occurred.

The importance of symbolical expression and of the pictorial presentation of religious facts and ideas has been confirmed, widened, and deepened both by the study of primitive cultures and religions and by the comparative study of world religions. Systems of symbols and pictures that are constituted in a certain ordered and determined relationship of the form, content, and intention of presentation are believed to be among the most important means of knowing and expressing religious facts. Such systems also contribute to the maintenance and strengthening of the relationships between man and the realm of the sacred or holy (the transcendent, spiritual dimension). The symbol is, in effect, the mediator, presence, and real (or intelligible) representation of the holy in certain conventional and standardized forms.

In its original meaning the symbol represented and communicated a coherent greater whole by means of a fractal. The fractal, as a sort of certificate, guaranteed the presence of the whole, and as a concise meaningful formula, indicated the larger context. The symbol is based, therefore, on the principle of complementation. The symbol, object, picture, sign, word, and gesture require the association of certain conscious ideas in order to fully express what is meant by them. To this extent, it has both an esoteric and an exoteric, or a veiling and a revealing, function. The discovery of its meaning presupposes a certain amount of active cooperation. As a rule, it is based on the convention of a group that agrees upon its meaning.

Religious Symbols and Iconography have been a part of humanity, and its seeking, from our earliest concepts of Self and identity, to the expression of those concepts, from our imagination faculty, to others.

There is an inner realm of vast information that Our symbolism and iconography explain in concise ways, forms, and patterns. This realm belongs to all of Us, and only a few share their perspectives, realizations, and overstandings.

The Universe encourages, and seeks to inspire, the expression of symbolic and iconographic interpretations that We call "Heights". These Heights come with meaning and definition to questions, circumstances, and dilemmas.

There are elements and components in symbolism and iconography that are important for identification, race value, and social interactions. Therefore, it is almost like a need is present for there to always be some form of symbolism and iconography, in society, expressed.

The regretfulness of this only arises when one group forces their particular symbolism and iconography, that helps them advance and elevate, on others who cannot benefit from the same symbolism and iconography. Let's take a look at a very emotionally charged subject in religion that proves this theory, and we'll start with an important question.

Does color, race, or any external characteristic matter in religious symbolism, iconography, their derivatives or associates?

There are always connections that exist in this world, though unknown, that need to be revealed, so that a clearer understanding can be had when investigating any subject. At this juncture, we want to explore large humanitarian, secular, and religious categories of importance defining what are the effects of symbolism, iconography, or any representation of conjured external characteristics, on people, and more importantly, how does it matter?

Our topic of inquiry will be the Eurocentric audiovisual symbolism, iconography and untutored phonography that is within contemporary Life, science, education, and religion: taking a look at Christianity; with emphasis on Yeshua (Jesus), the Anointed, who has been illiterately taught to be the crude Greco-Roman deity created between the 4th and 6th centuries, and constructed through the proceeding millennium into the form and phonation observable today.

We do not presently have the availability to fully expound an exegesis on Our topic chosen, for it is to vast to be done so in this present writing, but, we will point to the relevant matters in its history and construction that do clarify crucial information that needs announcement at this time. We will reveal a better understanding of what Our total body of work wishes to convey; and that is how external, objectified imagination, called symbolism, iconography, imagery, idolatry, and phonography, has a role and affects a role ubiquitous, in people, their communities, and interactions with others, even if unadministered.

Thereafter, we will define the components and mechanisms that allow symbols, icons, images, etc., etc., to be perceived and furthered into perceptions, which is the process, act, or faculty of recognition and interpretation of sensory stimulation based chiefly on memory; stemming from the mental, neurological, processes by which such recognition and interpretations are effected. All of this altering our insight, intuition, and knowledge of the Truth of this world.

    First and foremost, lets dig into the definition of Symbols in the Religious Consciousness, and how Man conjures up what it is and makes it. Secondly, we will address the symbol and how it relates to the sacred, and how they become indicators of the sacred or holy. Thirdly, we want to see what the sacred is in time and space, and don't worry we'll leave physics, to some degree, out of this version. Next, we will point out ceremonial and ritualistic objects as indicators or bearers of the sacred or holy; and then we will venture into how symbols, and their visual audio family are constructed, debated, confirmed, and canonized into Christianity. Do not see our use of predominant Christian examples as we being against Christian Ideology, it's just that Christianity has such a depth of study available for almost any topic we Homo Sapiens wish to discuss. Christianity's wealth of knowledge and information on Humanity, and our development, sociology, psychology, etc., is priceless to all subjects inquired of by man, allowing for a parallel to be maintained when exploring multiple topics simultaneously.

    The formation of religious symbols that occur when unconscious ideas are aroused or when a process of consciousness occurs is principally a matter of religious experience. Such symbols usually become intellectual acquisitions, and, as religious concepts are further elaborated upon, the symbols may even finally become subjects of major theological questions. In Christian theology, for example, summaries of dogmatic statements of faith are called symbols (e.g., the Apostles', Nicene, and Athanasian creeds and the confessional books of Protestantism, such as the Augsburg Confession of Lutheranism). This particular use of the term symbol is exceptional, however.

In the development of the symbol, religious experience, understanding, and logic are all connected, but each place has different accents on the individual categories and species of symbol. Occasionally, religion is regarded as the origin and the product of certain established (or fundamental) symbols. In such cases the outcome of the process of the structuralization of religious consciousness would then be the establishment of a symbol that is generally applicable to a particular historical species of religion. Conversely, one could ask whether the experience and establishment of an individual or collective symbol by a creative personality or a community is not itself the establishment of a religion. If so, the classical symbol that was developed at the time of the foundation of any one particular religion would then be constitutive for its origin and further development (e.g., the T'ai Chi or the combination of Yin and Yang for the Chinese, the cross for the Christian religion). In any event, the symbol belongs to the essence of man's coming of religious consciousness and to the formation of history's institutional religions. It plays a fundamental and continual part in the further growing of such religions and in the mental horizons of their followers.

Whatever the experience of reality that lies behind the religious symbol may be, it is, above all, the experience of the sacred or holy, which belongs essentially to any concept of religion. The historical study of religions has shown that it is fundamentally the symbol that mediates and forms, for man's religious consciousness, the reality and the claim of the holy. Religion is a system of relationships, a system of reciprocal challenges and responses; the principal correspondents of which are the sacred or holy and man. Though there are many forms of experience in which the sacred or holy is distinctly known and felt, the experience is often acquired in worship, in which this system of relationships is realized and continually renewed, and in which the sacred or holy supposedly makes itself present. The details of worship serve to objectify and regulate, in a perceptual and material manner, the presupposed presence of the sacred or holy, of which the symbol and the picture are intended to be its materialization. In its material manifestation, the sacred or holy is adapted to man's perceptual and conceptual faculties. Viewed from the aspect of its holiness, the symbol originates in a process of meditation and revelation, and every encounter with it is supposed to bring about a renewed actualization and a continual remembrance of this revelation.

The actualization of the presence of the holy by means of symbolic representation can, in extreme cases, lead to an identification of the physical manifestations with the spiritual power symbolized in them. The symbol, or at least an aspect of it, is then viewed as the incarnated presence of the holy. The sacred stone, animal, plant, drum and the totem symbol or the picture of ancestors, all represent the sacred or holy and guarantee its presence and efficacy. The origin of many such symbols clearly indicates that the identity that was presumed to have existed between the symbol and the sacred or holy actually does. The Greek god Dionysus as a bull, the Greek goddess Demeter as an ear of corn, the Roman god Jupiter as a stone, the Syrian god Tammuz-Adonis as a plant, and the Egyptian god Horus as a falcon all are viewed as manifestations of the deities that were originally identified with as these respective objects of nature.

The symbol is understood to have a referential character. It refers to the reality of the sacred or holy that is somewhat and somehow present. When the symbol is an indicator of the sacred or holy, a certain distance exists between them, and there is no claim that the two are identical. Short of actual identification, various degrees of intensity exist between the symbol and the spiritual reality of the sacred or holy. The symbol is a transparency, a signal, and a sign leading to the sacred or holy. The objects, gestures, formulas, and words used in meditation, for example, the Buddhist mudras (gestures), pratimas (images), mantras (formulas); and in mysticism, for example, the crystal or the shoemaker's ball in the contemplative experience of Jacob Bohme, a 16th- to 17th-century German cobbler and mystic; the navel in Omphalicism (a method [called Hesychasm) of contemplating the navel in order to experience the divine light and glory in medieval Greek Christian mysticism of the monks of Mt. Athos); the pictures of the deity in the language of Hindu; Islamic, and medieval Christian mysticism, are truly symbols. But nonetheless they have at most only an indirect mediating relationship to the divine, a purely noetic (intellectually abstract) significance with regard to the reality and presence of the sacred or holy.

The symbolical forms of representation of the sacred or holy are to be understood as references to or transparencies of the sacred or holy. The sacred manifests itself in time and space, so that time and space themselves become diaphanous indications of the holy. The holy place-a shrine, forest grove, temple, church, or other area of worship-is symbolically marked off as a sacred area. The signs, such as a stake, post, or pillar, that delimit the area themselves are endowed with sacred symbolic meanings, which often can be noted by their particular designs. The ground plan of the sacred building and its orientation, walls, roof, and arches are all utilized to symbolize the sacred or holy. Prehistoric places of worship- e.g., Stonehenge (in England) and other megaliths of Europe and the shrines and holy places of ancient Egypt, Babylon, China, and Mexico-were invested with symbolical meanings.

Sacred places are often pictorial reflections of the universe and its design and partake of its holiness. The domes of Christian churches are symbols of heaven, the alter a symbol of Christ, the Holy of Holies of the Temple in Jerusalem a symbol of Yahweh, the Holy of Holies in Shinto shrines (honden) a symbol of the divinity, and the prayer niches in mosques a symbol of the presence of Allah. In many instances shoes may not be worn on holy ground (e.g., Shinto temples), and hands and feet are to be washed before entering into a holy place. The woodwork of demolished Shinto shrines, when taken to private homes, makes the sacred or holy present in the homes of pious Japanese families.

Time as a transparent symbol of the sacred may be represented by means of the cycle of the sacred year and its high points e.g., New Year's (as in ancient Near Eastern religions), the times of sowing and reaping, and the solstices and equinoxes. Or the lapse of time may be represented in signs and pictures. Cosmic, mythical, and liturgical time and destiny are portrayed, for example, in the Buddhist symbol of the wheel of life, bhava-cakra, with its causal chain of human deeds and succession of existences, entwined by the claws of a devouring monster. The figures of Aion (Time) in late Greco-Roman and Persian antiquity show a figure with a winged lion's head standing on a globe and encircled by a snake. Time itself, its course, division, and fixed points, is both an allusion and the bearer and mediator of the sacred or holy.

Liturgical and ceremonial objects can also indicate or lead to the sacred or holy. Not only holy pictures and symbols (e.g., the cross in Christianity or the mirror in Japanese Shinto) but also lights, candles, lamps, vessels for holy materials, liturgical books, holy writings, vestments, and sacred ornaments are indicators of the sacred or holy. Liturgical vestments and masks are intended to transform the wearer, to remove him from the realm of the this-worldly, and to adapt him to the sphere of the sacred or holy; they help him to come into contact with the divine-for example, by obscuring his sexual characteristics. The vestments may be covered with symbols, such as those worn by Arctic shamans (medicine men with psychic transformation abilities). They are signs of the function of the wearer and his relationships to the sacred or holy and to the profane world. Such vestments are frequently derived from those of rulers or from ceremonial court dress; e. g., Japanese Shinto and Roman Catholic and Eastern Orthodox Christianity. They are supposed to create a fitting atmosphere of solemnity and dignity. In Western Christianity, the liturgical vestments have a very specific symbolism: the alb (a tunic) symbolizes purity of heart; the stole, the raiment of immortality; and the chasuble (an outer Eucharistic, or holy communion, vestment), the yoke of Christ. The liturgical vestments of the Eastern Christian churches have a similar symbolism. The ritual headdress and the crown express the sacred dignity of the wearer. The vestments of the various religious orders (Oriental and Occidental) express the holiness of the members of the community, their nearness to the sacred or holy, and the significance of religious life for them. In the reception ritual of Jainism and Buddhism, the monastic vestments are put on as a sign of an entrance in a new state of life. This ritual in Jainism resembles that of a wedding ceremony. The taking over of the monastic grab is an essential part of becoming a sadhu. The monks of the Jainistic Svetambara sect wear five objects (e.g., shells) as symbols of the five monastic virtues. In early Christianity, the white baptismal vestment was a symbol of rebirth, new life, and innocence.

Up and into the eighteenth century, the Four Gospels were constructed, narrated, defined and harmonized, i.e. dovetailed, together to form a single picture of Yeshua (Jesus). The church would argue that this was done in order to teach Christianity to the illiterate easily. Nevertheless, the Historical Yeshua (Jesus) has only an indirect relationship to contemporary Christianity and its questions, with the material being subservient to the western evangelists' purposes. It is now required of Us to cause a distinction between fact and value, between history and faith, so that Truth can finally be revealed. The only way this can be done is by determining what's defined by the church's symbolism, iconography, imagery, and phonography, and its effects on people, individually and collectively, we will start at the core of Christianity's Majority lead belief system, which at this present time, is not Christ at all.

At its initiation, Christianity was not Christianity, it was not Judaism, and it wasn't any of the Protestant denominations that exist today. At its initiation, Christianity was Israelitic Hebraism, typical of the Essences of the 4-1 centuries B. C..

The Semitic language was still in use, but heavy Greek influence was becoming recognizable. Characteristics of Greek thought and culture were being introduced to those inhabitants who were brought in as captives a few centuries earlier. This infusion of Greek thought, culture, and knowledge will eventually find its full manifestation in the centuries after the Advent of Yeshua and His Teachings labeled as Christianity.

Neuroscience tells Us that the neuronic and synapse response to Our thoughts, over time, become so real, it's as if they materialize right into this world. So that means that many people do not really have faith or believe anything that evolves and grow, but do have a very good neuro connectivity and synapse activity to the memory of a teaching that is now embedded into their brains. Therefore, it is not their hearts that are leading them, guiding them, but rather the neuro functions talking to themselves; compiling, assimilating, and storing a cohesion of comfort that soothes the interactions of the individual to his environment (An environment can lead to a belief in something just as powerful as any spiritual revelation can). Meaning, we can take on unnatural conditions and states just because We live or even daily interact in a place.

    The early church was one full of Life and diversity. Each location satisfied the needs of those it served, in the region that they lived, according to their culture and environment. It was spiritual in the sense that neither harbored any ill will towards any other for what was being presented in helping the needs of those people it saved; because not all people have the same needs and requirements at the same exact time, if at all. So diversity was mandated by geographical and demographical standards. The mind-set at that time was one that said that; so long as there is a uniform foundation, the growth and development should be allowed, with only the requirement of Truth. For it is only One God, and One Heaven that All Seek. Elevation is the goal of spirituality.

    Everyone has two distinct perceptions of themselves, internal and external. The external is concrete, it is what it is, and without cosmetic surgery, we either accept it or not. It's aesthetic, and We only wish that those around Us accept it as beauty or appealing. But the internal is a whole 'nother entity indeed. It is rooted in our thoughts of value, worth, the sublime, and how our beliefs are constructed by them. If any other measure of those elements are given from a different perspective, if any of those concepts aren't defined in a way that is aligned with what We feel is true of Ourselves, then We will hate Ourselves as is, and not even know it. We will then strive to assimilate something or someone, other than what's true for Us, into Our psyche and being. In other words, We will believe everything that suits a comfort of how facultative and facilitative Our internal perception is towards that. And while the external perception can be overcome with minimal adjustments or trends, the internal perception requires the greatest of efforts. For it is stored in the Subconscious Mind of how one feels concerning themselves. The essential nature of things affects Us there, so it is only through erudition and application of essential knowledge that a correction can ever be made. Just believing is not enough when what you believe isn't suited, conditioned or favorable towards your interest or benefit.

As the French would say "Del' aucace, en core del' sudance, et toujours del'audence" (Audacity, more audacity, and even more audacity).

The devil is in the details, because anytime the devil does a thing it is elaborated with pomp and circumstances. For this subject, Our pomp and circumstance will be several Ecumenical Councils. In these councils, elements were added and components were constructed for the eradication of established Truths; and their replacement with the introduction of anthropic doctrines. The events leading to a schism were not exclusively theological in nature. Cultural, political and linguistic differences were often mixed with the theological. Any narrative of the schism which emphasizes one at the expense of the other will be fragmentary.

What were initiated as Ecumenical Councils were the attempts of the Religious and Political Powers to manipulate facts, truths, beliefs, and faiths, into an orthodox consensus, and establish a coherent Roman Empire. This coherency could only be concretized when the man known as Yeshua ben Yoseph was elevated to divine status. The process for this elevation and anointing began in 325 A.D. with the First Council of Nicaea, which enunciated the Nicene Creed. This creed states:

"We believe in one God, the Father Almighty, maker of all things, both visible and invisible; and in one Lord, Yesus the Christ, the Son of God, Only begotten of the Father, that is to say, of the substance of the Father, God of God and Light of Light, very God of very God, begotten, not made, being of one substance with the Father, by whom all things were made, both things in heaven and things on earth; who, for us men and for our salvation, came down and was made flesh, was made man, suffered, and rose again on the third day, went up into the heavens and is to come again to judge both the quick and the dead; and in the Holy Ghost."

Here is where separation was wedged between the Creator and His Creation which came forth from Him; where the separation of thought began; and where the nascent of Procrustean Doctrine invaded Christ's Teachings. In Genesis, the created things brought forth "after their kind" and "after his kind," but man, male and female were created in God's own image (so God created man in his own image, in the image of God created He him; male and female created He them. Genesis 1: 27). So all of man possessed this Innate

Greatness, until the First Council of Nicaea; where it was removed from Man and given to a man.

There is Great Debate as to how much of God dwells in Man. We are made from His Image and Likeness, and He Blew the Breath of Life into Man, creating a Living Soul; but we still ponder on the remnants of those acts of Creation; we still wonder if anything is left.

That curiosity, of the Divine Presence in Man, was greatly injured in the First Ecumenical Council. Giving the position of "Same Substance with God" to only One Man propelled everyone else into an obfuscatory state within themselves. Whatever good that religion could have hoped to accomplish, began to deteriorate with this new information spreading. And with the inculcation of this knowledge, religion almost guaranteed the success of wickedness and unrighteousness. A people who sees God as separate from themselves certainly aren't prepared to do His will in their lives unceasingly. This is the underlying Truth of this council's canon setting. A look out at the landscape of Christianity now reveals the contrast that was seeded in 325 A.D.

The mire that came from that one canon caused the obdurateness of Christians, in allowing the same revelation that elevated Judaism to Christianity, with the Advent of their Messias, to happen again or with any other religion. They concretized this way of thinking with their iconolatry, and later their phonography, of names, places, and things they deemed sacred.

A second canon continued what the first canon announced by denouncing Arianism, the belief that the Son of God did not always exist, but was created, and is therefore distinct from God the Father. This is the cementing of the ideology in the deification of their version of Yeshua, in which the Greco-Roman culture is well familiar with, and always does to its prominent figures of history, making him more than anyone else could ever be. The Council of Nicaea dealt primarily with the issue of the deity of Christ. The ideal of The Trinity, which was being spoken of over a century earlier in the writings of Origen (185- 254) and Tertullian (160-220), and a general notion of a "divine three" was recognized, but wasn't doctrine level in a more full-fledged form until the Council of Constantinople in 360 A.D. It is here that the fantasy of Christ has its nascency.

The deification of Yeshua continued in the other councils that followed. The council of Constantinople (381 A.D.) confirmed the First Council of Nicaea's denouncing of Arianism, the belief that the Son of God didn't always exist. The First Council of Ephesus (431 A.D.) declared Mary, the mother of Yeshua as Theotokos (Mother of God or God-Bearer). The Council of Chalcedon (451 A.D.) declared that Yeshua is both truly God and Truly Man. These are just some of the emissaries that the Early Church cemented as ecclesiological of Christianity, but a major step in the deification of Yeshua, and a deviation from Truth, was yet to come.

Imagery and Iconography have been a part of the human experience for tens of thousands of years. There is a deep calling in our species to replicate the things around us, and even things that aren't perceivable here (beyond the sense recognition of the human being).

From the first to the seventh century, debate and argument was constant in either allowing icons or not allowing them. In the 8th century it came down to sides, in an all-out war. The iconoclast soldiers lead violent protests to keep these images out of the church. But, by 786 both sides were tearing at the fabric of Christianity's unresolved early traditions.

In that same year (786) Constantine VI and Irene announced an imperial edict, for a council, to be had in the summer, to unite the church which had schismed from a previous council in 754 over icons. The Synod of Hieria confirmed Iconoclasm, which was a movement within the Byzantine church to establish that the Christian culture of portraits of the family of Christ, Mary, the Saints, subsequent Christian, and biblical scenes were not of a Christian origin, and was therefore heretical and idolatry.

Iconoclasts destroyed much of the Christian churches' art history, which is needed in addressing the traditional interruptions of the Christian faith and the artistic works that in the early church were devoted to Yeshua the Christ or God. Many Glorious works were destroyed during this period (Two prototypes of icons would be the Christ Pantocrator and the Icon of the Hodegetria). In Catholicism, the tradition of icons have been seen as the veneration of "graven images" or against "no graven images." From the Orthodox point of view graven then would be engraved or carved. Thus, this restriction would include many of the ornaments that Moses was commanded to create in the passages right after the commandment was given, i.e., the carving of the cherubim. The commandment as understood by such context interpretation would mean "no carved images." This would include the cross and other holy artifacts. The commandment among the Orthodox is understood that the people of God are not to create idols and then worship them. This was forgotten, then fought, then overruled, so that a "Ruling" could be manifested. Next is a summary of the events bringing the world to this place.

The 2nd Council of Nicaea met for the first time on August 1, 786, in the presence of Emperor Constantine VI and Empress Irene. The proceedings were interrupted by the violent entry of iconoclast soldiers, faithful to the memory of Emperor Constantine V (741-775), the council was adjourned until the arrival of a reliable army. It didn't assemble at Nicaea again until September 24, 787.

After eight sessions, an enunciation was decreed and proclaimed with 22 canons.

Second Council of Nicaea (787 A.D.)

* Byzantine Iconoclasm - the practice of destroying icons and images. This council repudiated this belief.

*Relics, part of the body of a saint or a venerated person, or else another type of ancient religious object, carefully preserved for purposes of veneration or as a tangible memorial. This council decreed that alters must contain a relic.

*Canon Law - body of laws, regulations, or disciplines made or adopted by ecclesiastical authority. 22 were issued by this council.

A synthesis of the Second Council of Nicaea and it's six recognized preceding councils:

The holy, great and universal synod, by the grace of God and by order of our pious and Christ-loving emperor and empress, Constantine and his mother Irene, assembled for the second time in the famous metropolis of the Nicaeans in the province of the Bithynians, in the holy church of God named after Wisdom, following the tradition of the catholic church, has decreed what is here laid down.

The one who granted us the light of recognizing him, the one who redeemed us from the darkness of idolatrous insanity, Christ our God, when he took for his bride his Holy Catholic Church, having no blemish or wrinkle, promised he would guard her and assured his holy disciples saying, "I am with you every day until the consummation of this age. The promise however he made not only to them but also to us, who thanks to them have come to believe in His name. To this gracious offer some people paid no attention, being hoodwinked by the treacherous foe, they abandoned the true line of reasoning; and setting themselves against the tradition of the catholic church they faltered in their grasp of the truth. As the proverbial saying puts it, "they turned askew the axles of their farm carts and gathered no harvest in their hands". Indeed they had the effrontery to criticize the beauty pleasing to God established in the holy monuments; they were priests in name, but not in reality. They were those of whom God calls out by prophecy, "many pastors have destroyed my vine, they have defiled my portion. For they followed unholy men and trusting to their own frenzies they calumniated the holy church, which Christ our God has espoused to himself, and they failed to distinguish the holy from the profane, asserting that the icons of our Lord and of his saints were no different from the wooden images of satanic idols".

Therefore, the Lord God, not bearing that what was subject to him should be destroyed by such a corruption, has by his good pleasure summoned us together through the divine diligence and decision of Constantine and Irene, our faithful emperor and empress, we who are those responsible for the priesthood everywhere, in order that the divinely inspired tradition of the catholic church should receive confirmation by a public decree. So having made investigation with all accuracy and having taken counsel, setting for our aim the truth, we neither diminish nor augment, but simply guard intact all that pertains to the catholic church.

Thus, following the six holy universal synods, in the first place that assembled in the famous metropolis of the Nicaeans ((1) Nicea I), and then that held after it in the imperial, God-guarded city: (i.e. (2) Constantinople I) We believe in one God… [the Nicene-Constantinopolitan creed follows]. We abominated and anathematize - Arius and those who think like him and share in his made error; also Macedonius and those with him, properly called the Pneumatomachi; we also confess our lady, the holy Mary, to be really and truly the God-bearer, because she gave birth in the flesh to Christ, one of the Trinity, our God, just as the first synod at (3) Ephesus decreed; it also expelled from the church Nestorius and those with him, because they were introducing a duality of persons. Along with these synods, we also confess the two natures of the one who became incarnate for our sake from the God-bearer without blemish, Mary the ever-virgin, recognizing that he is perfect God and perfect man, as the synod at (4) Chalcedon also proclaimed, when it drove from the divine precinct the foul-mouthed Eutyches and Dioscorus. We reject along with them Severus Peter and their interconnected band with their many blasphemies, in whose company we anathematize the mythical speculations of Origen, Evagrius and Didymus, as did the fifth synod, that assembled at (5) Constantinople. Further we declare that there are two wills and principles of action, in accordance with what is proper to each of the natures in Christ, in the way that the sixth synod, that at (6) Constantinople, proclaimed, when it also publicly rejected Serhius, Honorius, Cyrus, Pyrrhus, Macarius, those uninterested in true holiness, and their likeminded followers.

A truncated synopsis of the 22 cannons reads:

We declare that we defend free from any innovations all the

* written

* unwritten

ecclesiastical traditions that have been entrusted to us.

One of these is the production of representational art; this is quite in harmony with the history of the spread of the gospel, as it provides confirmation that the becoming man of the Word of God was real and not just imaginary, and as it brings us a similar benefit. For, things that mutually illustrate one another undoubtedly possess one another's message.

Given this state of affairs and stepping out as though on the royal highway, following as we are

* the God-spoken teaching of our holy fathers and

* the tradition of the catholic church--

for we recognize that this tradition comes from the holy Spirit who

dwells in her-- we decree with full precision and care that,

* like the figure of the honored and life-giving cross,

* the revered and holy images,

* whether painted or

* made of mosaic

are to be exposed

*in the holy churches of God,

*on sacred instruments and vestments,

*on walls and panels,

*in houses and by public ways,

these are the images of

*our Lord, God and saviour, Jesus Christ, and of

*our Lady without blemish, the bold God-bearer, and or

*the revered angels and of

*any of the saintly holy men.

The more frequently they are seen in representational art, the more are those who see them drawn to remember and long for those who serve as models, and to pay these images the tribute of salutation and respectful veneration. Certainly, this is not the full adoration (latria) in accordance with our faith, which is properly paid only to the divine nature, but it resembles that given to the figure of the honored and life-giving cross, and also to the holy books of the gospels and to other sacred cult objects. Further, people are drawn to honor these images with the offering of incense and lights, as we piously established by ancient custom. Indeed, the honor paid to an image traverses it, reaching the model, and he who venerates the image, venerates the person represented in that image.

* So it is that the teaching of our holy father is strengthened, namely, the tradition of the catholic church which has received the gospel from one end of the earth to the other.

* So it is that we really follow Paul, who spoke in Christ, and the entire divine apostolic group and the holiness of the fathers, clinging fast to the traditions which we have received.

* So it is that we sing out with the prophets the hymns of victory to the church: Rejoice exceedingly O daughter of Zion, proclaim O daughter of Jerusalem; enjoy your happiness and gladness with a full heart. The Lord has removed away from you the injustices of your enemies, you have been redeemed from the hand of your foes. The Lord the King is in your midst, you will never more see evil, and peace will be upon you for time eternal.

Therefore all those who dare to think to teach anything different, or who follow the accursed heretics in rejecting ecclesiastical traditions, or who devise innovations, or who spurn anything entrusted to the church (whether it be the gospel or the figure of the cross or any example of representational art or any martyr's holy relic), or who fabricate perverted and evil prejudices against cherishing any of the lawful traditions of the catholic church, or who secularize the sacred objects and saintly monasteries, we order that they be suspended if they are bishops or clerics, and excommunicated if they are monks or lay people.

Anathemas concerning holy images

1. If anyone does not confess that Christ our God can be represented in His humanity, let him be anathema.

2. If anyone does not accept representation in art of evangelical scenes, let him be anathema.

3. If anyone does not salute such representations as standing for the Lord and His saints, let him be anathema.

4. If anyone rejects any written or unwritten Tradition of the Church, let him be anathema.

The definition and canons summarized here point out how representative art, iconography, and imagery was brought into the church, into this religion, which previously held a standard of achieving high spirituality through concentrated effort. There was no need for anything external if "the kingdom is within thee". But again, while most attempt to see symbolism, imagery, and iconography as simple additions to an effort of spiritual elevation, it is when that effort is accompanied by an underlying bias or prejudice that it does more harm than good.

Representative art is exponentially more than just what the artist, patron, or benefactor believes in, it is what they also see of themselves, their identity, and their position in the world. And if that position is one of arrogance, pride, or ignorance of inclusion and union, then that representative art becomes oppressive, weighty, and overwhelming to others whose identity or culture is not of that and/or different.

In the now common representational art of the Christ, His Mother, the Saints, or any biblical, religious scenery, most every other cultural identity has been excluded and/or permanently removed. This was done with the great effort of the Church, and its Eurocentric ideal of supremacy. This notion of superiority infected the Church's purity and was doctrinally defended, defined and explained through the two eras of Iconoclasm (image breaking) 730-787 and 813-843, to its own injury of separation and division.

In order to have something established, and able to stand the test of time, maintenance must be regular so that what is wanted remains. The church maintained this position of arrogance. Not only did images become venerated, but they well reflected the bogus ideal of a superior race, and that therefore made her tyrannical.

And even as recent as 1994, their doctrinal defense has been repeated in her catechism. It reads in part; The sacred image, the liturgical icon, principally represents Christ. It cannot represent the invisible and incomprehensible God, but the incarnation of the Son of God has ushered in a new "economy" of images:

Previously God, who has neither a body nor a face, absolutely could not be represented by an image. But now that he has made himself visible in the flesh and has lived with man, I can make an image of what I have seen of God… and contemplate the glory of the Lord, his face unveiled.

Christian iconography expresses in images the same Gospel message that Scripture communicates by words. Image and word illuminate each other:

We declare that we preserve intact all the written and unwritten traditions of the Church which have been entrusted to us. One of these traditions consists in the production of representational artwork, which accords with the history of the preaching of the Gospel. For it confirms that the incarnation of the Word of God was real and not imaginary, and to our benefit as well, for realities that illustrate each other undoubtedly reflect each other's meaning.

All the signs in the liturgical celebrations are related to Christ: as are sacred images of the holy Mother of God and of the saints as well. They truly signify Christ, who is glorified in them. They make manifest the "cloud of witnesses" who continue to participate in the salvation of the world and to whom we are united, above all in sacramental celebrations. Through their icons, it is man "in the image of God," finally transfigured "into his likeness," who is revealed to our faith. So too are the angels, who also are recapitulated in Christ:

Following the divinely inspired teaching of our holy Fathers and the tradition of the Catholic Church (for we know that this tradition comes from the Holy Spirit who dwells in her) we rightly define with full certainty and correctness that, like the figure of the precious and life-giving cross, venerable and holy images of our Lord and God and Savior, Jesus Christ, our inviolate Lady, the holy Mother of God, and the venerated angels, all the saints and the just, whether painted or made of mosaic or another suitable material, are to be exhibited in the holy churches of God, on scared vessels and vestments, walls and panels, in houses and on streets.

And in a rousing conclusive statement, the Church says: "The beauty of the images moves me to contemplation, as a meadow delights the eyes and subtly infuses the soul with the glory of God." Similarly, the contemplation of sacred icons, united with meditation on the Word of God and the singing of liturgical hymns, enters into harmony of the signs of celebration so that the mystery celebrated is imprinted in the heart's memory and is then expressed in the new life of the faithful", the Catholic Catechism.

We have defined the components and elements of what can be perceived. The subject and topics have been expounded on, to a degree, for clarity. The narratives point out usage and intent by individuals and groups. We have presented a sample of the initiation, continuation, and defense in allowing imagery, iconography, phonography, and symbology into worship; since the religious category has the clearest and most common of recognizable examples. So now we want to investigate and elaborate on the entity that Our previous writing takes its effect in, and on, and that is the Mind. We need to know what the Mind is, so that we can really grasp the significance of Our observation of objective and subjective works.

Everything around Us, we perceive as a mental stimulus of some sort. This means that there is a measurable quantification of our mental operations, because of our environment. The knowledge of where these quantified measures end up, and effect, is valuable to the person who wishes to "safeguard" his reality. Understanding the design elements, structure and components assists, with the sentinel purpose. No one should have a mind that is unprotected, or leave their minds unguarded.

The things that are identifiable by the titles symbolism, iconography, phonography, ect., are first and foremost mental. They were conjured up from the mental. They first happened in a mind, and they affect and conclude with a mind. The applications they trigger are maintained by the mind also. Therefore, we will shift our journey over to the Mind, its definitions and philosophy, in order to know why "Perceptions" be what they are.

The mind makes things real, it makes things our "Reality". Its work is to assimilate the individual to his subjective and objective worlds, and it will do this by any means necessary, with anything available. With this going on 24/7, the inner workings of the Mind is required to further the understanding of the probable weaponry of symbolism, iconography, imagery, and phonography.

It is often maintained that the essential nature of the mental consists of states, or degrees, of consciousness in a person. After anesthetics or a temporary loss of consciousness, a host of experiences of color and light, sounds, feelings, thoughts, and memories flood in on him. As far as his objective, observable, behavior is concerned, he may be lying unmoved and unmoving. But as far as his state of consciousness is concerned, he may be undergoing a series of subjective experiences. To show an example of this, think of when one perceives the glow of a golden piece of material. He experiences the homogeneous, spread-out, distinctive goldenness present before him. A blind or color-blind person who has never experienced "golden" would not have the awareness of "goldenness" that the normally-sighted person has. What he has and what the blind person lacks is something that philosophers have called "Raw Feel". It's a peculiar and special way that looking at something "Feels".

The subjective experience of the golden is to be contrasted with the discrimination of golden things. We could imagine a blind person who is about to discriminate golden from other colors by use of optical instruments (e. g., spectroscopes with Braille printouts), but he would lack the subjective experience of the color; he would not know that look of golden. Defenders of this view would claim that there is a great variety of subjective experiences, and that the experience of colors is only one of them. Sensations (e.g., the experience of pain, tickles, throbbings, pangs, nausea, and tiredness) provide another such example.

Still other subjective experiences include: the experiencing of images, after images, memory images, and others; feelings of exultation, depression, pride, anger, fear, and love; and thought- imaginings, surmisings, doubting, and recollectings. All of these episodes, occur at a particular time and place, in which the subject is in a state of awareness that has a particular content, as seen when observing some objective form. This is the initial point of affect that the "Perception" of a thing begins to be seeded.

The question now arises of how adequate subjective experience is as a criterion of the mental-whether, though it is obviously a sufficient condition for something to be mental, is it a sufficient condition for something to have a mind. A perspective on this is had when we ask the question of whether a creature that has but one state of consciousness could be said to have a mind; the popular view is that it could not. This view says that it takes, at the very least, a number of states of consciousness, linked by memory, before one would say that the creature had a mind; and it may be that there has to be a certain level of complexity in the nature and relation of the conscious states, for there to be a mind. It is doubtful, however, whether consciousness is a necessary condition for the mental.

Now, to answer our question, based on the effects observed in religious symbolism, subjective experience not only affects the mental, but is a sufficient condition for something to be said to have a mind. Subjective experience is where the mechanisms of the philosophy of mind nascents, and after some time, evolves into practicle applicable manifestations and materializations.

We have so much confusion about symbols, images, ect., because we have so much confusion about the mind. There are a myriad of descriptions, phenomenon, noumenon, and cognitive functions that no one considers when dealing with this physical world. The sciences of psychology, psychiatry, and all of their derivatives, came into existence to try and grasp the subjects of the mental and mind. So it's no wonder that the average person doesn't know the way that either is affected, especially the effects of symbols, iconography, images, and phonography.

Before Sigmund Freud, it would have been widely agreed that the notion of unconscious mental phenomena was logically impossible, a contradiction in the very terms. That view had one important exception however, in Gottfried Wilhelm Leibniz, a 17th century Rationalist and mathematician. He held that there are "petite perceptions" of which the subject is unconscious. They are so slight, so similar to others, so familiar, or in such a crowd of other perceptions, that the subject is unaware of them at the time. An example would be becoming use to the sound of an elevated train, a fire station, or waterfall near your house. Leibniz seemed to have in mind what modern psychologists call "Subliminal Perceptions".

Subliminal Perceptions are those below the threshold of awareness, but still capable of leaving some effect on the mind. This is where the mischievous manipulation can come in. Religions are first in the usage of subliminal perceptions as a tool, and as a weapon. Governments are a close second in applying it, & corporations, through advertisements and product placement, use it to facilitate profits.

It was Frued's great contribution in discovering a range of phenomena of which the patient was unconscious but which were very much like typically mental phenomena, especially in the behavioral manifestations that gave power and ability to manipulators, oppressors, and subjugators. In the light of such similarities, of conscious and unconscious phenomena, it was plausible to extend the concept of the mental to include these unconscious phenomena, especially since they were such that the patient could become conscious of them through hypnosis or psychotherapy, which reinforced the reaction to the stimuli through daily interactions and observations. Freud postulated a mechanism that he called "repression" to explain why the patient is unconscious of them. This repression is defined as the unconscious exclusion of painful impulses, desires, or fears from the conscious mind. Meaning simply, that you make it a part of your identity that you do not want to actually confess to, but that does find expression in your behavior.

In addition to the subliminal and the unconscious, there are more familiar characteristically mental phenomena that do not consist of states of consciousness. When a man falls into a dreamless sleep, he does not lose all his beliefs or abandon all his goals, he does not cease wanting a better world or being artistic or imaginative or lazy, nor does he forget how to do arithmetic or speak French. A person is not jealous of someone only when thinking of him, nor does a businessman have confidence in the dollar only when concentrating on business. Obviously, these mental characteristics can apply in a dispositional way to people who are not at that moment expressing or exhibiting that disposition. That is just how powerful, and convincing, the mind is in applying an idea of the world.

So with this sample of information, what is being stated? Well, what's being stated is that Perceptions are the makeup of people. All that we come in contact with as a stimuli is assimilated into one wonderful homogenous view. Whatever is in that view, whatever is observed with any intent, triggers the relative action. It all matters because it is how we are made. Whether a person introspects or retrospects (the truth appears to be that sometimes he does the one, sometimes the other) he would still seem to have a knowledge about his own present and recently past mental states that reveal every degree of stimuli; oppression, elevation, denial, Love, hate, agreement, ect., ect.

There are states in life that are necessary for us to grow and develop. They are our assisters in our advancements in all phases of our lives. But they should only be used for that advancement. They are not supposed to be permanent fixtures of our identity, or the identity of our collective. Making them permanent and unchanging, un-evolving, actually harms those who possess the knowledge of their existence, instead of benefitting them. We lose the ability to discern transmitting from receiving. This brings us to the problem of the mind, the will, and action.

Intellect and emotion often come to expression in volition and action: important topics in the philosophy of mind-topics that comprise such concepts as motives, desire and purpose, deliberation, decision, intention, attempts, and action, both voluntary and involuntary.

There is a rough distinction to be made between the things that happen to a person and the things he does or makes to happen. If a person slips on the ice, it is something that happens to him, if he walks on the ice, it is something that he does. "Henry slid on the ice" is ambiguous; it may report something that happened to Henry or something that Henry did, depending upon the meaning. In this example, the observable event may be the same; from a photograph of Henry sliding on the ice one may not be able to tell which it is. The problem of action is primarily to understand this distinction and its ramification. Wittgenstein once put the question this way: 'And the problem arises: what is left over if I subtract the fact that my arm goes up from the fact that I raise my arm?"

There are a number of different answers: (1) Actions are events produced by causes of certain sorts-volitions or acts of will according to some theories; beliefs and desires under other theories; and simply persons or agents in yet another theory. (2) Actions are events that are "caused" in a special sense; they have a teleological rather than an efficient or mechanical cause, or an immanent (or originating) cause rather than one that is merely a reaction to, or modification of, an action coming from some other source. (3) Actions are events that are properly characterized and assessed in terms of rules of conduct, or principles of rational and ethical behavior, and for which the agent is held responsible, liable, accountable, to be praised or blamed, rewarded or punished.

Any theory of actions is expected to throw light on the issue of free will, a matter of great importance for ethical theory. If the philosopher holds that free will is compatible with determinism, any of the views above will allow for free will. Even if he holds that an action is not free if it has causes that eventually lie outside the agent, his view will be compatible with the various views of action unless he holds the version of (1) -that an action is an event produced by volitions or beliefs and desires-and also holds the additional thesis (2)-that volitions or beliefs and desires themselves have causes that lie outside the agent. Only then will there be no freedom of the will.

I want to interject something here, before we move on. This something has to do with causes that lie outside of an agent. This outside is not necessarily external of the person. The outside that we are referring to is only outside the focal consciousness or immediacy of our attention.

The human brain contains as many nerve cells as there are stars in the Milky Way, and that number is in the billions. Blind sight, partly, how emotions travel from person to person, is a deeply buried subconscious sensory system rooted in a hidden part of the brain that receives signals from the eyes only when the image is loaded with emotions. Visual Emotions travel to the Amygdala, the Superior Collicus and six other structures in the brain. That makes us more connected to what we don't know than what we do.

The human visual system consists at least of nine (9) different pathways. We are only beginning to understand One. The other eight are completely in the background. There are subconscious mental pathways that allow us not to see emotional stimuli but to sense them. We all have them, but they are normally overwhelmed by our primary sense of sight.

Our brains can sense things even when we are not aware of them. This implies that any search for a kind of "Sixth Sense" depends on understanding the boundary between conscious awareness and subconscious experience.

To understand consciousness is to think of it in layers-layers constructed from the data our sense are gathering. Consciousness has all these different levels. First of all, there's primary consciousness. This is consciousness of the things around you. You see what's around you, that's the first level, but then if we were to stop and reflect, we could be conscious of our consciousness. We can become conscious of what we are thinking about. Then we've got consciousness within consciousness. If we reflect even deeper, we can start to be conscious of the fact that we are conscious of our consciousness. Then we got consciousness, that contains consciousness, that contains consciousness. Going three levels deep. In principle, you could repeat this to infinity, and this would certainly qualify to some as outside of an agent, but is well known to be within.

Some things are in the background of our consciousness, way out in the distance. Some things are flickering through our consciousness grabbing our attention for a moment, then they move on. Some things are in the focus of our consciousness. They grab our attention and hold us in suspense. They do not let us go. So, since our brains are dealing with so many layers of function and operation, it stands to reason that we might not be aware of everything we are sensing. Some measurable cognitive activity goes unnoticed, but does have effects that eventually reveals themselves.

In the mid 1980's there was an investigation into a strange phenomenon. Readouts of electronic devices called random-number generators were being affected by people sitting next to them if those people focused their thoughts on them. Random-number generators are electronic coin tosses.

But, instead of heads or tails, they throw ones or zeros. Their results are supposed to be totally random, hence their name.

In the 1990' s, an experiment was set up to confirm if people could change randomness. It was called the Global Consciousness Project. It ran 24 hours seven days a week, collecting data and sending it back to a lab in Princeton. With 340 independent experiments, done over a 12-year span, the data strongly suggests, with odds of a billion to one, that there is such a thing as a collective consciousness (or global mind). This also means that things that happens to one, conjured by one, or done by one has a deep inner knowing by others, and can stir them to actions. All of this is happening in the realm of subjective experience, and the intent here could be projecting from an unknown source, which we will call a field.

Fields are regions of influence. We see this readily with magnetic fields in their repelling or attraction of each other. They do this because of a self-organizing property in the field. Fields are inherently integrative, and one that scientist have now attributed to man is called a Morphic Field. Morphic Fields organize the bodies of animals and plants and organize the activities of brains and minds. It allows birds to fly in a perfect formation, guides mass migrations of herd animals, and it is the reason we get that creepy feeling when someone stares at us. This suggestion states that our minds work through extended fields that stretch out far beyond our heads into the world around us, linking us to other people and to our environment, internally.

Morphic Fields are more commonly known as the Sixth Sense. The sixth sense is effectively the ability to detect information at a distance-that's one of the definitions-through mechanisms not known to date. Think of it like this, Earth's magnetic field is like an ocean rippling with waves. Electrical activity from our brains can surf along on top of it, passing from one person to another, or one group to another.

Human thoughts are not non-physical. They are in the brain itself. And, under certain conditions, they can be transmitted across space. All seven-plus billion human brains are immersed, and encompassed, by the Earth's Magnetic Field, which is wave like. A change in one, if it's connected, and we are, causes the magnetic flux line to go right through us, right through our brains. This could change one, who would then change those closest to him, and then, that initial change in one could influence everyone.

But our senses may not just be able to travel across space. They may be able to reach out across time and feel the future or our past. And believe it or not, human consciousness does not just react to a major event, it is an inextricable part of them.

There is an experiment that I wanna share right now. The experiment is called The Presentiment Experiment. It is a way of seeing whether or not, in principle, that sometimes we are getting our future experience. Presentiment has shown, for decades, that we can respond to things before they appear to us. They call it Presentiment Response, and right now it's measured to be about five seconds, but they don't know what the limit is.

I know that this interjection, as well as the subject matter itself gets technical at times, but it is necessary, and will all come together.

In the 1950's it was realized by renowned physicist Richard Feynman that James C. Maxwell's theory of light and electromagnetism equations had bizarre advanced waves, solutions that allow us to see the future, information traveling from future to present, an opposite direction to us. Could this alternate solution to one of the basic laws of physics explain some of the strange phenomenon we hear about and read about? And overall, can it help explain how/why the affects and effects of iconic, symbolic, and phonographic stimuli take precedence with us? I pose these questions because it is said that "light created the eye", so what are signs, imagery, and symbols creating?

Well, I don't want to cloud any opinion on our discussion and defining of our subjects and topics. But what I will do now, is shift to a study on precognition and premonition, by professor Daryl Bem of Cornell University, that gives even more clarity to what affects and effects Us and what is going on with us, so that we are well aware of it.

Professor Bem's study states that we use our sixth sense for evolutionary, reproductive purposes, the ability to sense erotic opportunities in the future; and that this has developed over millions of years. It was shaped by evolution to give individuals an edge in finding mates.

Now I know that many of us don't like "evolutionary" talk, but I use it here to stay true to the study that also points out the things that we need in this writing to complete the overall thought of Perceptions.

To continue with the findings suggested by the professor's study, we see that evolution rides on reproductive advantage. So it makes sense evolutionarily to think that precognition or something like it would certainly serve reproductive advantage and survival advantage. Precognition and premonition reveals that time may not flow neatly in one direction, and humans, being evolutionary survivors, have learned to use that to their advantage, even unknowingly, and even in ways not designed for the use of. Professor Bem calls it "feeling the future" because it tries to get in the fact that the future is able to affect your thoughts, cognition, and emotions.

So in summary, we have a sense about things that may be future or past, we know that this sense is tied to small amounts of energy, it tells us of a connection between everything. We have anomalous findings, that says that it doesn't fit into the current structure of how we conceptualize physical reality. But we have evidence of its existence in the way that we live and the way that others live around us. We know that we are only looking at the edge of psychic phenomena. And therefore, only know the tiniest power of the mind.

So where are we, as individuals, in all of this? What is symbolism, iconography, phonography, etc., to us? Can we determine its affects, its effects? Do we know the functions of the substrate of the mind, the brain, and how these relate to the mind, searches for remedies, healings, or cures for anything that is outside of us, yet manifests inwardly, only to then reveal itself outwardly again, but in a different expression? What is all of this, and what does all of this means in the "Grand Scheme of Things"?

Evaluating the psychogenic from the somatogenic, and determining the factual or truth to any of our individual and collective expressions, will create a diagnosis that would explain the necessary steps that need to be taken so that betterment and the elevation of a "Being" can be produced. It would point out the injuries from those things that are harmful to us, and prescribe what would allow us to avoid any further harm in the future.

We have to become better people while on this Earth, and knowing that there are stimulates acting on us in a myriad of ways, especially cognitively, will assist us in doing so. Knowing the psychodynamics of ourselves from the effects of symbolism, icongography, imagery, phonography, and idolatry grants us an advantage over the happenstance ways of these entities in our lives. Structure, organization, and calculation would expand our own control and benefit us in our own lives.

Heed must be taken in this day and time. There will not be one of us successful in Life if we continue ignoring what's going on around us, with us, and to us. Those forty (40) still shots that our visual system takes every second is filling Our minds with information, symbols, images, etc., that move us, shake us, and points us in directions that sometimes takes years for us to realize we're going in, and that that direction is wrong for us.

We have surely become more knowledgeable in neuroscience, of how the mental, physical, and spiritual, are all present; and are all related, interact, and are interdependent, not independent of each other, in our psychobiology and psychoculture. We must now make a powerful push towards coalescing this knowledge with the spiritual in order to initiate a Global Panacean Commonwealth, and remove our conflicts at their sources and origins. This we can do, but we have to know how we are going to do it. We have to know why we are going to do it. We have to know "Intent".

One attribute that sharply distinguishes man from the rest of nature is his highly-developed capacity for thought, feeling, and deliberate action. Here and there in other animals, rudiments, approximations, and limited elements of this capacity may occasionally be found; but the full-blown development that is called mind, that proposes his "Intent", is unmatched elsewhere in nature.

Understanding "Intent" involves analyzing those concepts that involve the mind, in an attempt to discover the nature of each of these concepts, the relations between them, how they are to be classified, and how they are to be related to certain other concepts; especially to the concepts of matter, energy, and the human experience. We will only summarize on these concepts, anything more than a summary wouldn't allow the completion of this book; such vastness is the nature of the Mind.

Intent, within the mind, in the technical sense, encompasses a variety of elements including sensation, and sense perception, feeling and emotion; dreams, traits of character and personality, the unconscious, and the volitional aspects of human life, as well as the more narrowly intellectual phenomena, such as thought, memory, and belief.

Now that we've pointed out our objective, let's describe "Intentionality", so that we are clear on what happens preceding that decision making moment, and why Our actions and behaviors become what they are.

Now, a way of explaining what is meant by "Intentionality" in the philosophical sense is this: it is that aspect of mental states or events that consists in their being of or about things (as pertains to the questions, 'What are you thinking of? and What are you thinking about?). Also, intentionality is the aboutness or directedness of mind (or states of mind) to things, objects, states of affairs, or events. To think at all is to think of or about something in this sense. Intentionality includes, and is sometimes taken to be equivalent to, what is called "mental representation".

It can seem that intentionality pervades mental life-perhaps it somehow constitutes what it is to have a mind. But achieving an articulate general understanding of intentionality presents an enormous challenge, like where is it, and what is its function, in the mind?

Intentionality is a characteristic of the mental. It is thought to be found in the certain ways in which an individual may be said to have something as his object. Thus, thinking, believing, desiring, and other such attitudes are thought to resemble one another in that they may be said to take an object, or to be directed upon an object, in a way quite unlike anything to be found in what is purely physical, this is intentionality. The concept has been emphasized by some of the Scholastics and was introduced to modern philosophy in 1874 by the German philosopher and psychologist, Franz Brentano, and clarified and defended by a U.S. philosopher, Roderick M. Chisholm, in the 20th century.

Intentionality is exhibited in a variety of phenomena. Thus, if a person experiences an emotion toward an object-e.g., loves, fears, pities, envies, or reverses it-he has intentional attitude towards it. Other examples of intentional attitudes towards an object are: looking for or expecting, believing in, doubting or conjecturing about, daydreaming, reminiscing, imagining, favoring, or disapproving a list that seems to go on endlessly. Because it clearly comprises so many of the things that one thinks of as typically mental, intentionality, being of broader scope than purposefulness, would seem to be a more appropriate choice then purposeful behavior for the criterion of the mental.

One of the characteristics of intentionality is what the scholastics called "inexistence". A man may be intentionally related to an object that does not exist or to an event that does not occur; which is why the symbolism and iconography of religion is such a powerful source of intent that we needed to comprehend. Thus, what a man looks for may not exist, and an event that he believes to occur may not occur at all (revelations, prophecies), and yet he places the utmost of his being on contemplating the actuality of it in his life and worship. In contrast with such a nonintentional phenomenon as bumping into something, in which the object bumped into must be real, looking for something (an intentional act) does not necessarily imply that the object looked for exist. Similarly, in contrast with an explosion's resulting in the fact that many were hurt, a witness's believing that many where hurt, (again an intentional act) does not imply the fact that many were hurt. Therefore, existence and Truth are irrelevant to intentionality.

Though this possible relationship to nonexistent objects as opposed to existent ones is a necessary feature of intentionality, it is not sufficient to define it, for there are phenomena that are equally concerned with nonexistent essences that are nonetheless nonintentional. "That man looks like bigfoot" may be a true sentence even if bigfoot, though having an essence, does not exist. Similarly, "The Sun will explode at temperatures about 100,000,000,000 degrees may be true whether or not such temperatures exist. So, intentionality requires further characterization if its scope is to be narrowed to exclude such examples as these. But, it does well in describing the relationship between man and things that he begins to have through sense perception.

Another characteristic of the intentional state is that not every description of its object will be appropriate. Not knowing that his belief is in, and a part of Abraham's religion, for example, a man may be in the intentional state of practicing Christianity, but not in a state of believing his faith is Abrahamic, similarly, he may believe in Christ as his Lord and Savior and yet not believe that Christianity's God is the exact same as Abraham's God. This second feature of intentionality, often called "referential opacity," is such that the true sentence asserting an intentional state will become false when some alternative description of the object of the state is substituted for it (it is false that he is practicing Abraham's faith).

Intentionality is a technical term in religion, psychology, and philosophy, it has a range of definitions showing that it stands for something familiar to us all: a characteristical feature of our mental states and experiences, especially evident in what we commonly call being "conscious" or "aware". As Sapient beings, or persons, we are not merely affected by the things in our environment, we are also conscious of these things; of physical objects and events, of our own selves and other people, of abstract objects such as numbers, and of anything else we bring before our minds. Most, if not all, of the events that make up our mental life-our thoughts, beliefs, hopes, fears, categorically "Perceptions"- have this characteristic feature of being "of" or "about" something and so gives us a sense of something in our lives. For example, when we see a house, our perception is a perception "of" a house; when we think that 5 + 3 = 8, we are thinking "of" or "about" certain numbers and a relation among them. When we hope that the world will one day coalesce, Our hopes is "about" a possible future state of the world, and so on. Each such mental state of experience is in this way a representation of something other then itself and so gives one a sense of something. This representational character of mind, awareness, or consciousness, its being "of" or "about" something, and we need to fully understand what that something is, is "Intentionality of Perceptions". We can go as far as saying that a relation between the mental state of the experiencer and, in typical cases, some extra-mental thing, event, or state of affairs (I have previously referred to these as "objects") are the Phenomenological Conceptions of Intentionality.

In a typical perception, the object that the perception is of or about, the one to which it's intentionally related, is the exact same object that causes the visual experience to come about. But, do not think of this as "Causal Relation, "or the more sophisticated" "Causal theory of Perception," because then intentionality could be regulated down to nothing peculiarly mental or just a matter of how the mind is externally related to ordinary sorts of extra-mental objects.

The problem, that is mentioned, with a relational view of Intentionality is that an intentional mental state or act is "Not" always some actually existing extra-mental object. We would have to apply a consciousness description, in the phenomenal sense, allowing the non-exiting mental state or act to "seem" to one some way, and some would call that deviating from a pure intentionality definition. But, in using intentionality to describe an aspect of Perceptions, intentionality has within it consciousness and/or awareness in the abstract realm of symbols, signs, icons, images, etc...

A thorough look at the historical, and evidencial, roots of controversies over consciousness and intentionality would take us farther into antiquity, and extremely off course of our subject and presentation then it is feasible to go in this writing, but do know that there is not yet any majority consensus made. Settling intentionality's controversies is not the subject nor the conclusion we are seeking. Our discussion is of Perceptions, and a portion of what intentionality is that deals with "inexistence".

This philosophical & phenomenal problem with intentionality's "inexistence" is what has revealed a fatal flaw in our social religious communities' doctrines and practices. Knowing that a relationship to some non-existing object is possible creates a major concern from a Seeking The Truth position and desire. I mean, is it not problematic to have a relation labeled "inexistence" when one of truth and existence "is" available? If one imagines a Minotaur, the half man, half bull, to whom young Athenian men and women were sacrificed in the Cretan Labyrinth, that is an act of imaginative representation "of" a Minotaur, and making a sacrifice means that one has a belief "about" a Minotaur. The "of" and "about" both qualify the state and act of the one, and his intentionality, even though the Minotaur is a purely imagined object. They do this because the intentionality of an act is independent of the existence of its object, even when it is related to something extra-mental. This feature is labeled "existence-independence".

This knowledge of existence-independence has become the weaponry of many different systems of our society, especially for religions and governments. Subtle and

Subliminal attacks on our person is being done through this particular pathway. Intentionality's purpose has been hijacked for another's gain, and with this done, we are nothing more than batteries, in similitude, if we don't recognize and make a serious change.

In making this accusation clear, let us describe existence-independence, and how its components can be used as weaponry. Existence-independence, within intentionality, means that intentionality has phenomenological (a science that can measure something known to the senses) properties (something that belongs to) in mental states or experiences. In simpler terms, it means that existence-independence has its own definition, in its own world, and is not concerned with how it is related to the external world, even if an act is directed towards an object that does exist in this world. When this is the case, the intentionality of the act changes with its internal character in ways that are independent of what is actually True of its object.

Let's look at this example of a weaponization and attack:

A group believes in God, they believe that He can manifest Himself, therefore they already have an inexistence and/or existence-independence intentionality of and about God. Now, if another inexistence and/or existence-independence object is wedged into the residence of the first, and is accompanied by the terror of physical and psychological abuse, and a manufactured ethnic deviant representation is conjectured and forcibly inculcated, that is a weaponization of intentionality and its inexistence/existence-independent elements, hijacking and imprisoning. The True Weapon of Mass and Matter Destruction of Babylon (Confusion).

There is no general agreement on the best way of conceiving of intentional phenomena. Brentano, at one point, thought of intentionality as being a relation between a subject and an entity, in which the entity is something that might or might not exist; but difficulties arise in characterizing the ontological status of such an entity i.e., it's kind of reality. More popular today are certain linguistic approaches: intentionality may be viewed, for example, as it was by Rudolf Carnap, a philosopher of science, and others, as a relation between a subject and a piece of language or, as others have explained, as a relation between a subject and a linguistic practice or linguistic role. Under this view, the intentionality consists not in the relation of a subject to an essence (that of Abrahamic) but in its relation to a sentence ("This is an Abrahamic faith") that has that alleged essence as its meaning. It remains to be seen whether such approaches will succeed in dealing with all intentional phenomena. It would seem to pose particular difficulty in those cases in which the intentional state is overtly directed toward some existent entity, with language playing a minor or null role, as in situations in which one feels anger, pity, or love toward someone; or when an animal is stalking its pray (which involves an intentional state). In such instances, an analysis in terms of linguistic attitudes would seem wide of the mark.

Digging a little deeper into the language of intentionality brings up the familiar term "Common Sense". I think here, in intentionality, "Common Sense" needs to be defined and described so that a clearer picture is painted on how intentionality erupts inside of Perceptions.

Common Sense will do well in taking us to the edge of actions and the depth of the reasons we perceive as we do. Knowing about the produced and engineered affects allows us, at this point, to fully comprehend the intent of symbols, images, icons, and phonography; and understand our own intentionality and how it's defined.

Taking a look from a religious perspective can give a clue to why Common Sense, in its original philosophical discussions, has such an actuating role in the Intentionality we exhibit.

Impoverished people respond to a vision of heaven as a large buffet that satisfies their physical needs. The faithful in the safety level of needs are predisposed to favor preachings about eternal security of the walls of the kingdom, Gods Presence, etc... Those who are fortunate enough to be above safety and security look down on those adherents as believers of "old religion". They only want the assurance that God is Love. A warm and Grandfatherly message like that would strike many worshipers in the esteem needs as self-indulgent. Faith to them means a sense of worth that comes from doing something of lasting value in God's Creation. Now to each group and their needs, the specific description and the approach of it towards their Intentionality and Perception will be legitimate, it will make Common Sense to them. But each will also look at the other groups approaches as ridiculous when viewed from above or sterile when viewed from below. This is where Common Sense needs to be understood as a "Social Climate" instead of a rhetorical tool.

"Common Sense" is the basic ability to perceive, understand, and judge things, which is shared by (common to) nearly all people and can reasonably be expected of nearly all people without any need for debate. The Merriam

Webster's Collegiate Dictionary, Tenth Edition, defines "Common Sense" as; The unreflective opinion of ordinary people: sound and prudent but often unsophisticated judgment. Rene Descarties, 17th century French philosopher and mathematician, who founded Analytic Geometry, and is well-known for his rationalistic premise, "I think, therefore I am", in the opening line of one of his most famous books, Discourse on Method, established the most common modern meaning, and its controversies, when he stated that everyone has a similar and sufficient amount of "common sense," but it is rarely used well. Therefore, a skeptical logical method described by Descartes needs to be followed, and common sense should not be overly relied upon.

The origin of the term, "Common Sense," stems from the works of Aristotle, the well-respected Greek Philosopher. His book, De Anima Book III, chapter 2, is where the most well-known definition arises. The passage is about how the animal mind, the physical, the sense of self, process sense-perceptions, memories and imagination, and converts their rawness, from the five specialized senses, into perceptions of real things, moving and changing, which create thought. Aristotle's understanding is that each of the five senses perceives one type of perceptible or sensible, which is specific to it. This "common sense" is distinct from basic sensory perception and from human rational thinking, but cooperates with both. As a sort of a summary, what "Common Sense" is saying is that it refers to a type of basic awareness and ability to judge, which most people are expected to share naturally, even if they cannot explain why. That's their inter-connected, complex, and evolved meaning, revolving around important political and philosophical debates in modern western civilization, notably concerning science, politics, and economics. To show the evolutionary journey of Common

Sense take notes of this: Aristotle placed "sensus communis" in the heart; Descartes placed it in the brain, in the pineal gland, but then, by 1649 and the issuance of his Passions of the Soul, he abandoned it as a faculty entirely.

The reason for bringing "Common Sense" forth in this section of intentionality, within Perceptions, is because it is where inexistence and existence-independence objects begin to be acted upon in addressing the "perception of needs" (and we will describe needs from the perspective of Abraham Maslow's Hierarchy, with our insight). We have discovered that what is common, in the sense and needs of one, is not the same as what is common in the sense and need of another.

What do we really know about "Needs"? Do we understand that the materialistic things are not the root need in and of itself? Are we able to comprehend that the house, car, woman, and God all speak to a place inside of us that satisfy core, fundamental, and essential needs? As he, that is the person in the experience, gets to be more purely and singly himself he is more able to fuse with the world; with what was formerly not-self. The I-thou monism becomes more possible, the creator becomes one with his work being created.

The states or categories of our "needs" have been titled, in one instance, by Abraham Maslow. Maslow's categorization is Physiological, Safety & Security, Social (Belonging), Esteem (Ego), and Self-Actualization. His word choice makes expounding on needs, within Intentionality, within Perceptions, readily comprehensible.

Physiological needs are physical survival needs, very basic needs, such as air, water, food, sleep, warmth, exercise, sex, yes sex, etc.. When these needs are not met or satisfied we will feel sickness, irritation, pain, and other discomforts. We are motivated to alleviate the adverse feelings, of not having these basics, with a sense of urgency, so that we establish homeostasis as soon as possible.

Safety and security needs are about establishing stability and consistency. These needs are mostly the beginning of satisfying psychological needs, or needs psychological in nature. Law and order comes to mind here, with the freedom from threats. Economic security that provides one with safe neighborhoods, good schools, and other community values are necessary to provide a safe and secured person.

Social needs are acceptance, love, sense of belonging, being a part of a group, or identification with a successful team. Clubs, work groups, religious groups, extended family, and even gangs provide for this need. Humans have deep desires to belong, feel loved, and be needed by others.

Esteem needs are very tricky indeed. There are two types of these needs. The first esteem need is one which results from being competence, skilled, or having a mastery of something. The second is the attention and recognition that comes from others about that competence, or those skills, or that mastery. This is similar to belonging, but it's about admiration and, to a degree, power. That's the tricky part. Once esteem gets to admiration and power it is Egoism.

These four needs can be agreed upon with a minimal discourse. But, number five, Self-Actualization, is not something everyone can agree is a "need". The desire to become more and more divine is not everyone's cup of tea. The longing to become greater than what one is, and to become "everything" that one is "capable" of becoming is to ask for a herculean effort or tremendous overcoming from oneself. One would have to take on challenging projects, opportunities for innovation and creativity, or learning and creating at a high level.

As we look out at T.V., the internet, especially social media, and any report of human activities in books, magazines or articles we should be saddened by the violence and inhuman deceit that are now normal communion behaviors. Lying, cheating, stealing, and murder are not what human nature was meant to be. These are aberrant behaviors, that occur when legitimate human needs are thwarted and unrealized.

The four "needs" that are described previously to Self-Actualization are Deficiency needs that must be satisfied before a person can act unselfishly. The upward climb is accomplished by satisfying one set of "needs" at a time. We're driven to satisfy the lower needs, but we're drawn to meet the higher ones. The lack that is created by "deficiency needs" creates a tension within us, and this is where the aberrant behavior and inhuman deceit stems from. Satisfying "needs" is healthy, blocking gratification makes us sick.

The urge to fulfill "needs" is potent but not overpowering. People can resist the pull of physiological, safety, love, and esteem needs, but it's not easy. Now, although everyone has the same set of "needs", the order can change, the description can be modified, or our ways of fulfilling those needs can be different. This is called, categorically, "The Prepotent Need". A prepotent need is the one that has the greatest power or influence over our actions. Everyone has a prepotent need, but the need will differ among individuals. One might be motivated by a craving for loving and another by a desire for esteem. The need that is prepotent for an individual is the lowest unmet need out of the four.

We can now see where common sense, and what it is saying to the individual, what is "common to" him, can dictate his perception, including his intentionality. Our surroundings, environments, communities, and demographics all play a role, affect, and influence how, what, and why we perceive as we do.

Now if we say that "Perceptions is Everything," what about that makes us who we are? Well, the process of forging an identity, of figuring out who it is we are, that's a process that really takes us our entire life time. Some of the most crucial parts of that are the things that we learn in a very, very, very early period of our lives. Our identity is not so solid when we are young. Most of our time, as children, is spent trying to figure out who we are. By the time, we become adults, we just accept who we were a minute ago, and keep trudging on. As kids, we were involved in this great existential, philosophical research program titled, "What it means to be a person".

One of the first milestones in this program is called "the mirror state". It begins when we recognize our own reflection. It connects you to your own kinesthetic feeling of yourself. At 15 months, most children aren't able to recognize themselves in a mirror. It is a big first step on a long journey of self-discovery, and also where we begin to associate with the environment that we are in.

The concept that there is a you, who is the same person even if your thoughts have changed, is not an understanding you're born with. It is something we come to learn at four years old. So a very important part of our identity is being able to say, when I was eighteen, I believed different things than I do now, but, that it was me who believed those different things. When as children we learn about the survival of our identities, that changes in our beliefs don't change who we are, we stop forgetting the things that we don't believe anymore, and for the first time unlock the astonishing power of human memory.

A lot of who we are is built upon the memories we make each and every day. Memories allow us to build these future simulations, granting us elements for building up that sense of who we are, but they can be manipulated without our even knowing it.

So are we really who we say we are, who we think we are? Our memory is remarkable. On average, we will grasp the meaning of one hundred thousand words (100,000), get to know around one thousand, seven hundred people (1,700), and read over one thousand books (1,000). From that vast and immense mental stores of experiences, we each build our own identity, a pattern of memories and their intensities, that are uniquely ours. The intensities of our memories, the ones that carry emotional weight, are allowed in, and given residence. The ones that don't are not.

Our memories are not just a record of the events that took place in our lives. They are malleable and fallible. Our identities are created with constant input from our society.

"No man is an island". So when we ask "Can we deliberately re-engineer someone's identity" the answer would be "Yes".

To do that we would need to peer at that person's inner most thoughts, and that technology is already here. We don't readily realize it, but all of our advancements in technologies secretly re-engineer who we are. The data input we receive from our devices and their signals alter, affect, and even change us. We start learning the languages, ideas, and even behaviors of what is being "uploaded" into our minds. All of this information causes us to act, and that acting is furthered by the time, people, and environment we share. We are all actors to some extent, who we appear to be can change, does change, depending on our mood or the company that we are keeping. But, there is one time though, when who we are really comes to the forefront, when we dream.

If we could see, or remember with great details, our dreams, and study them, we could know ourselves in a more profound way than ever before. During an average life span, a person spends about six years dreaming. That's more than 52,000 hours of imagery buzzing through our unconscious brains. That imagery, what it is, what it means, and what it's going to do has a tremendous effect on our identity. Those unconscious aspects of our mind define what we are and what our identity is. Like it or not, our memories shape how we think and how we act, and that's revealed in our dreams. What makes us who we are, or what makes our identities are bits from our memories, our dreams, and our imagination. No one's sense of self is truly and permanently fixed. Our Perceptions are measured and calculated in ways, levels, and degrees that we have yet to fully understand. But hopefully, now we all will begin to.

"Perceptions Is Everything" is not in itself an unavoidable conclusive thing. A person can conclude whatever they think of themselves, never-the-less will still have perceptions as part of their daily existence. As we've just said, in our dreams we become exactly who we truly, fundamentally are, and that person is a mosaic of his perceptions and beliefs as he comprehends them. Most of the time this is being done on a very subconscious level. I say "very subconscious" because it is nearly an instinctual mechanism.

Knowing about how we perceive, what we perceive, and the internalization, is a very powerful ability. It protects the potential you and keeps you on course. Realizing that there are people, places, things, and systems that affect Perceptions, and then feed off of our Perceptions, is an important defense against manipulation.

Looking around, we can see so many invented signs, symbols, images, and sounds. They all project out from a deep internal place, and extend out into the world for operation and/or machination. Done on an individual, one one one, person to person level, it can be seen as simple or complex manipulation; depending on what is the objective that is hoped to be achieved. Done by groups, organizations, corporations, or government, it is Machiavellian and paints the world in an abstruse way. Understand what is received in your Perception. It is, and will be, "Everything" to you.

****

The Dissonant's Slave

Quick to run and do what he say,

You are the dissonant's slave.

If you harm one of your black sisters or brothers,

You are the dissonant's slave.

Calling beautiful black queens bitches and hoes,

You are the dissonant's slave.

Not caring for your sons and daughters,

You are the dissent's slave.

Not listening to your spiritual, and physical Mother &

Father, You are the dissonant's slave.

Refusing to assist in the rise of the beautiful Black African

Nation, You are the dissonant's slave.

Looking at our black sisters and brothers in Africa

Different from yourself,

You are the dissonant's slave.

Promoting separatism amongst people of color,

You are the dissonant's slave.

Destroying one another and stagnating the advancement

of our people,

You are the dissonant's slave.

Start coalescing and stop being the dissonant's slave by
Loving thyself and thy people,
You are not the dissonant's slave!!

****

Anointing my crown to keep my mind & thoughts in a
righteous & pure state. Anointing my feet every day, so
that my path may be
cleared of any snare that is before me is providence.
Anointing, on daily journey, is for keeping spiritual
wickedness in high places in check, and, away from
breaching or intruding on the
sanctums, mind, body, and atman.
To be sanctified with prayer oil is providence and
Spiritual protection for InI and InI loved ones.
The sanctity of prayer oil is causing the wicked ones to
Reveal themselves in abominable ways.
InI and the two wendem anoint everyday as we trod the
Belly of the Beast, and, coalesce as the trinity in the way
of life. Paying homage to the atman with prayer oil and
incense in introspection.

****

All, things in this universe know that they are a part of
the Most High's Oneness, and therefore give their praises

and Performs rituals all the time.

Even nature performs its rituals of oneness, the great Rock standing still, Is being obedient to displaying its power. The great waters gives life and washes away all impurities, and does the wave dance.

The great trees, including the Tree of Life, give shade and feeds knowledge of good and corrects evil. The wind blowing is a ritual.

Awaking from sleep is a ritual.

Thinking is also a ritual.

The soil and the yielding of its fruits is performing a ritual.

Walking is a ritual, etc.

****

The cyber world and the technology is poisoning the minds & atman of the children and world with pollution and non-attunement with there atman. This way of life is not in alignment with the natural way of life, this causes families to not have the proper relationships. We need to realign and be obedient to the Universal Law with power in place and in order; with the Supreme Universal Self. Not cybernetics or devices and the vice that they upload into our atman.

Let's start observing everything with Subtle Spectacles. All of nature, like the sun, moon, and stars are being obedient and are in alignment with Divine Universal Law.

****

Thoughts are like a marathon; the mind will run a marathon if you let it. Control your thoughts and mind by passing the baton in the race of positive vibrations. What emotion controls your decision on what's right & wrong, positive or negative, and where do they come from within you? Do your desire come from a place of love?

A place where Supreme Love dwells is where our feelings for what is right or wrong comes from. The thoughts create the emotion that create the feelings which causes the vibrations of positive and negative.

Observe your thoughts and feed them with food from the divine. The observer needs to feel the mind in its essences, Good Positive Vibrations.

A mind with G. P. V. seeds or Divine Food will not and does not harvest anything that's not divine.

Physics says that energy cannot be created or destroyed, but it can be converted. So let us convert this energy that's within

everything and everyone, so that the Supreme Universal Self can be realized.

Aquarius, give life to all the other ages as well as the Stardust called life.

Ras Jah GoGo

The Ulotrichous'sPrayer

I love thee O'thy darkness,

O'thy voidness, and thy blackness.

Let InI give thanks and praise to thy one true self within, there is beauty and goodness in melanin.

Grateful, Faithful, and Truthful is its color in thy sight.

O'thy beginning of all vibrant colors, let the Star of Africa shine within. Rise O'thy origin of man's heart ulotrichous's, be

proud O' beautiful ulotrichous one.

Maven in coalescing with the inner rainbow of love and life. O'thou of great valor and rectitude, let the introspection that is needed be given to InI by the strong arm of providence.

O'thy darkness, and voidness let Jah Black-Light come and continue to shine in InI forever more Amen.

Ras Jah GoGo

****

Perception of A Mom

Mirror mimics, beautiful to display the unique

For it shows what lies Beneath, for Diamond Girl.

Curved just right; glare within

the darkest night. She knows what it takes to expand the

brand of Diamond Girl.

It takes that stain of coal, the

temperature of Mars, the time of

a Goddess, and the grace of unity,

for Diamond Girl.

Overtime, glamour multiplies, Look up

Look Down, they're rubies, they're pearls,

they're crystals and gem stones, gold to

support those all for Diamond Girl.

Remember jewels are passed down,

So if she plucked you, show off yourself

to everyone downtown, but let them know

you came from uptown, from a Diamond Angel.

Your Son,

by: Douglas Jean

******

Perception of A Wombman

It is with the highest appreciation that I present myself, in Spirit, to those who are gathered together in order to celebrate the Elevation of an Angel. My Angel was brought here in February of 1978 eleven months after I arrived in March of 1977. Causing us both to be born under the sign of Pisces; a match We physically met in the seventh grade, and all I could see was her beauty, her light. She proved to be smart, caring, and spiritual, and she affected me in the most profound ways. When our Son was born, little did I know that her shear will would make him my own role model. In fact, all of our kids bare markings of her unimaginable Love that she has for them, it's in the Love that they themselves have for each other. They are manifestation of her Spirit being caring, smart, and Spiritual. To know her is to adore her. Her friendship is not part-time or temporary. What she gives you is a gift for life. Through troubling times or times of joy you knew that you had her support & comfort. She is the true definition of a wife, that's a fact. For me, no one can truly take her place, and they won't be able to, because she will always be here in spirit. It's that spirit that's eternal, and there is where she has her peace, so will we all. I thank you all for attending this celebration of Life. May the peace of God expand within Us all.

Ras Jah GoGo

RASTAFARI PERCEPTION

RITUALS

A representation of natural symbol of life's nature and sacred to them performing Rituals.

attack oN Human beings and the world

These our the many devices and cybernetics, symbols

Ulot
ulotrichous's
ulotrichous's

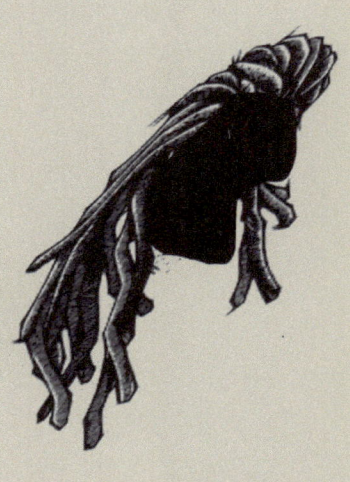

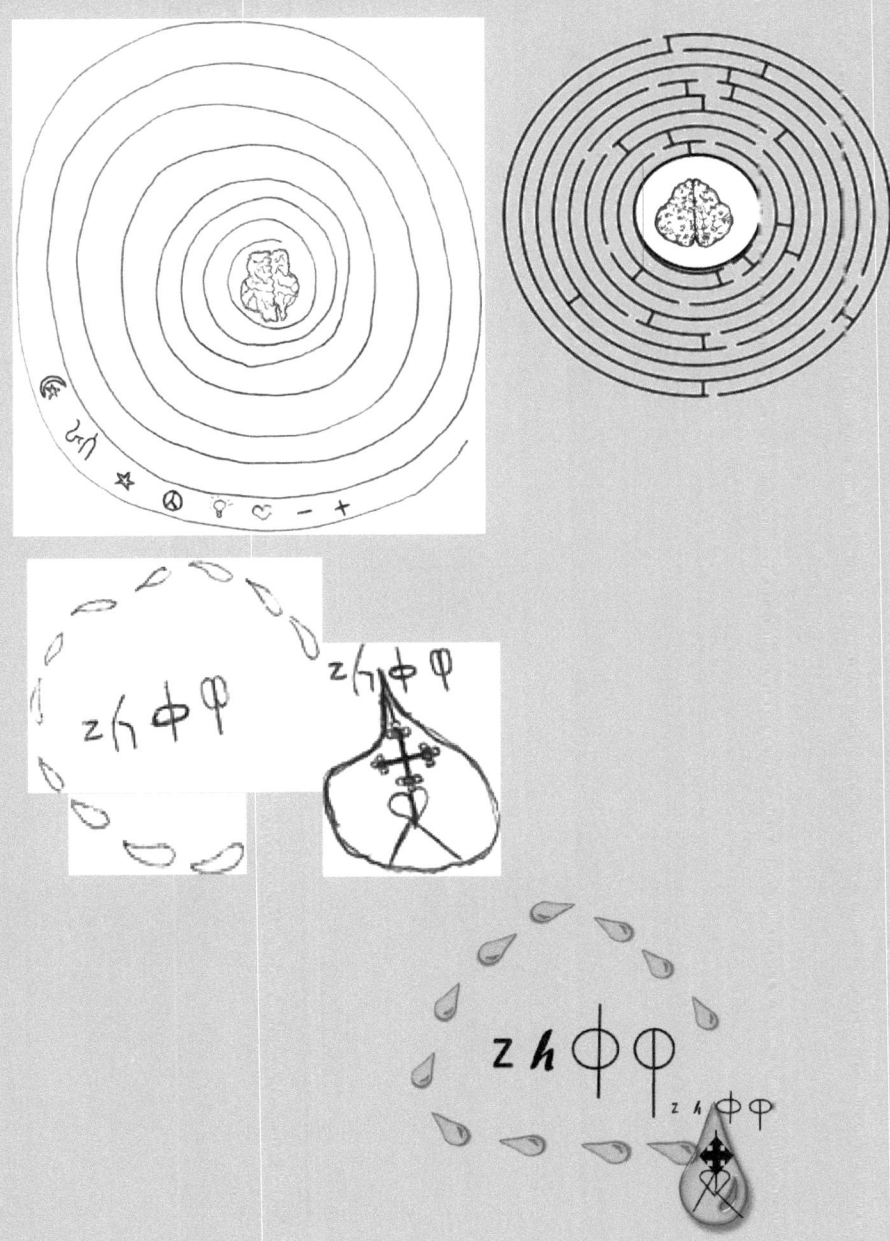

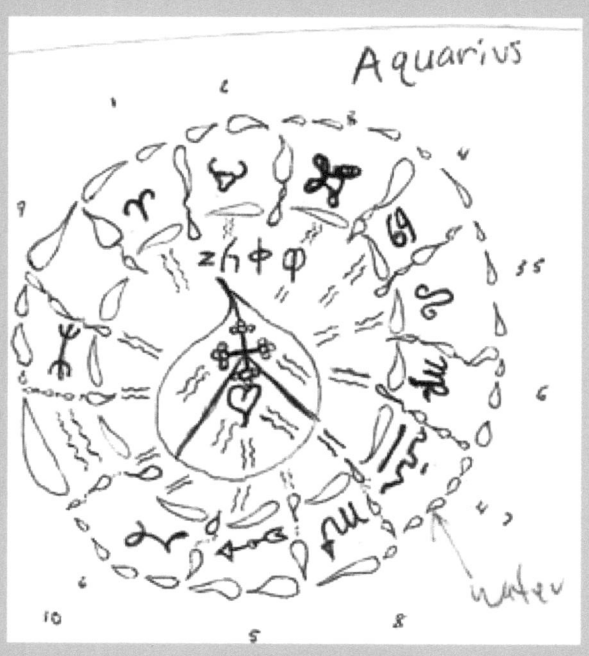

Hindu Om (or Aum)

This is the most universal of Hindu symbols and sound is used in meditation. In Hinduism, the word "Om" is the first syllable in any prayer. More specifically, Om is used to symbolize the universe and the ultimate reality. Some people say that this symbol represents the three aspects of God: The Brahma (A), the Vishny (U) and Siva (M).

Chinese

Earth - In ancient Chinese texts, the Earth Element was often depicted as the center with the other four elements surrounding it.

Earth provides nourishment and shelter for all life. The Earth Element and its two officials, the Spleen and Stomach, are the organs that support the nourishing processes in body, mind, and spirit. The stomach takes in nourishment; the spleen distributes the energy throughout the body obtained from foods.

Egyptian

KA

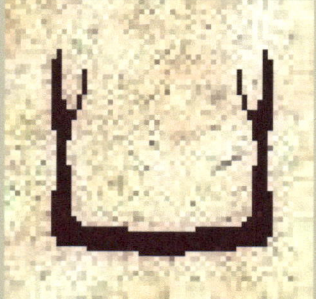

The ka is usually translated as "soul" or "spirit" The ka came into existence when an individual was born. It was believed that the ram-headed god Khnum crafted the ka on his potter's wheel at a person's birth. It was thought that when someone died they "met their ka". A person's ka would live on after their body had died. Some tombs included model houses as the ka needed a place to live. Offerings of food and drink would be left at the tomb entrance so the ka could eat and drink.

Greek

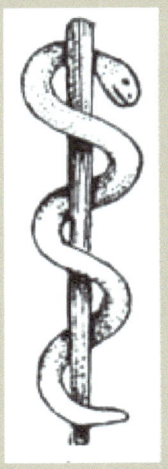 The asclepius wand, or asclepius rod is is an ancient Greek symbol associated with astrology and with healing the sick through medicine. The rod of Asclepius symbolizes the healing arts by combining the serpent, which in shedding its skin is a symbol of rebirth and fertility, with the staff, a symbol of authority befitting the god of Medicine. The snake wrapped around the staff is widely claimed to be a species of rat snake, Elaphe longissima, also known as the Aesculapian or Asclepian snake. It is native to southeastern Europe, Asia Minor, and some central European spa regions, apparently brought there by Romans for their healing properties.

Budist

Swastika - In the Buddhist tradition, the swastika symbolizes the feet or footprints of the Buddha and is often used to mark the beginning of texts. Modern Tibetan Buddhism uses it as a clothing decoration. With the spread of Buddhism, it has passed into the iconography of China and Japan where it has been used to denote plurality, abundance, prosperity and long life.

Origin of the Peace Sign

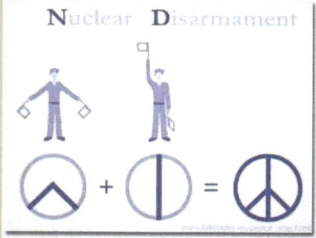

Originally, it was an image of a dude slumped over in despair. Gerald Holtom, a British graphic designer, came up with the peace sign design in 1958 to be used at a protest against nuclear weapons. It's actually a kind of double entendre: People have adopted one interpretation of the symbol, two superimposed semaphore letters -- N and D -- which were meant to stand for "nuclear disarmament. "But what we've forgotten was the primary image that Holtom was trying to portray: In his own words, his logo was meant to be a "human being in despair." The inspirational peace sign is in actuality a representation of a man who has lost hope in a world gone mad, stretching his arms out and downward in desperation and defeat.

HAMSA HAND

The hand-shaped amulet with an eye at the center of its palm is used mostly in Arabic cultures as a protection against the evil eye. It's also known as the Hand of Fatima, for Mohammad's daughter, and as the Hand of Miriam in Judaism, for the sister of Moses. The Open Hand had been used in ancient cultures: in Buddhism, the open hand signifies that all points of the teaching are visible, while in Hinduism, the downward pointed open hand signifies "giving."

Basically, Taiji is a concept to illustrate the evolving process of the universe itself and everything in the universe from Wuji (origin) to Taiji. Or it is the ultimate Dao (truth or principle), which includes Yin/Yang and all other principles and things. Taiji involves Yin/Yang (Liangyi), then evolves to Sixiang (from Liangyi), then Bagua (from Sixiang) -- another important Chinese ancient idea.

The circle of the Taiji picture represents one, universe or Wuji. The black and white part indicate Yin and Yang (or Earth and Heaven), respectively. The curve boundary between the black and white represents everything or the human world between Yin and Yang (or Earth and Heaven), and the curve stands for change and interaction. The white dot in the black part shows some Yang exists in Yin and the black dot in the white part shows Yang contains some Yin. Thus, Yin and Yang are not mutually exclusive and static. They are constantly evolving or changing to create the colorful universe.

The Taiji concept is first from Yi Jīng (or I Ching) -- a Chinese classic. Taiji (Yin/Yang) has been rooted in many aspects of people's daily life, such as Taiji Quan (shadowboxing) and Chinese medicine

Alchemy wasn't just a quest to transform lead into gold: it was a quest to transform base things into greater, more spiritual things, including the elevation of the soul. Alchemists coded their notes in a variety of personalized symbols.

A young goldsmith gave Claddagh ring to his lover and promised to marry her. However, before the wedlock, he was kidnapped by pirates. His love, refused to believe that he was killed and was never to come back. She waited for five years, until one day he escaped, made a fortune and returned to his love for live happily ever after. Ever since that time, Claddagh ring has been an ancient Irish symbol of love and commitment. The ring bears the design of two hands clasping a heart and a crown on top. It's a popular symbol of friendship and eternal love. This Irish symbol depicts romantic love, platonic love, promises, commitments and forever.

 **Acorn luck symbol** - The acorn is considered to be an emblem of good luck, prosperity, youthfulness and power, the acorn is a good luck symbol. The acorn may often also represent spiritual growth. The Norse believed that acorns displayed on a windowsill would protect a house from lightening. This may seem somewhat trivial to many of us today but back in the day it was a widely-accepted idea.

Hecate`s Wheel

This labyrinth-like symbol has origins in Greek legend, where Hecate was known as a guardian of the crossroads before she evolved into a goddess of magic and sorcery.

Hecate's Wheel is a symbol used by some traditions of Wicca. It seems to be most popular among feminist traditions, and represents the three aspects of the Goddess Maiden, Mother and Crone.

Ethiopian crosses are almost invariably made from elaborate lattice work. Hand-held crosses usually include a square at the base, which represents the Ark of the Covenant, and both the Ark and the Cross bear the Shekinah (see Prince of Peace Cross). Geometric patterns are common in Ethiopian art and there is order and meaning in the intertwined lattice style. This represents everlasting life and also relates to the nature of the Ethiopian Orthodox Church.

Instead of imploring the world to "give me your tired, your poor", the Statue of Liberty's welcoming message might well have been "as-salamu alaykum", the Arabic greeting used by Muslims around the world. That's right, the world's most recognized symbol of freedom and the American dream, was originally intended for Egypt, which ultimately rejected it for being too old

fashioned. The decision came as a disappointment to Lady Liberty's creator, Frédéric Auguste Bartholdi, who'd envisioned the Suez Canal as the ideal venue for his mammoth harbor structure.

XMAS

Xmas is a common abbreviation of the word Christmas. It is sometimes pronounced /ˈɛksməs/, but Xmas, and variants such as Xtemass, originated as handwriting abbreviations for the typical pronunciation /ˈkrɪsməs/. The "X" comes from the Greek letter Chi, which is the first letter of the Greek word Χριστός, which in English is "Christ".[1] The "-mas" part is from the Latin-derived Old English word for Mass. There is a common belief that the word Xmas stems from a secular attempt to remove the religious tradition from Christmas by taking the "Christ" out of "Christmas", but its use dates back to the 16th century.

OLYMPIC RINGS

The five Olympic rings symbolize the union in sports of Africa, America, Asia, Europe, and Oceania. The colors represent competing nations. (One color was on each nation's flag when the rings were conceived in 1913.)

MERCEDES BENZ

The three-pointed star in the Mercedes-Benz logo reportedly came from inventor Gottlieb Daimler's dream of building motor vehicles for land, air, and sea.

But the star itself is an ancient symbol. For thousands of years, stars have oriented humans wandering in the darkness. The star represents something inside of us that is visionary, starlike. It is a symbol of the Self — a higher part of us — of wisdom, guidance, and destiny. Mercedes owners are guided by this symbol whenever they get behind the wheel.

THUNDERBIRD

A mythical Native American creature that dominates all natural activities, the Thunderbird symbolizes divine dominion, protection, provision, strength, authority, and indomitable spirit. This cross-cultural symbol is found among the plains Indians as well as the tribes in the Pacific Northwest and Northeast, though its meaning may vary across different groups. Some tribes considered the Thunderbird to be a sign of war and the sound of thunder in the clouds was believed to be a prophecy of victory in tribal wars if ritual dances and ceremonies were performed. Others looked at the Thunderbird as a solar animal that controlled the dawn of day and night by opening and closing its eyes that were made of the Sun.

Caban

This ancient Mayan symbol is representative of the Earth keeper who sanctifies the Earth and venerates all life that exists on it. Reminding everyone of the larger forces that are behind all creation, this Earth symbol represents movement, transition and synchronization. It motivates people to be patient, observant and flexible. It also symbolizes the synergistic working of destiny that brings everyone together for shared spiritual intents. Focusing on the Caban symbol helps one become centered and experience spiritual unfolding.

Pikorua

- This is a Maori twist symbol that resembles an intertwined new-growth pikopiko fern frond found in the damp woods of New Zealand. It represents the beauty, strength and endurance of the bond of loyal friendship between two people. It is also symbolic of the crisscrossing and inter-linked paths of life of friends. True friends share an eternal connection that will not weaken even when the persons are separated at times. Pendants inspired by this symbol are often gifted to friends in celebration of a lasting and loving relationship.

www.ingramcontent.com/pod-product-compliance
Lightning Source LLC
Chambersburg PA
CBHW042334150426
43194CB00005B/161